Praise for *Inbound Selling*

"*Inbound Selling* is a handbook for organizations, managers, and sales professionals who are ready to adapt to a world where the buyer is in control and competition is closing in.

As a first-time salesperson and sales manager, a top performer and studious learner, Signorelli provides a first-person account of his years inside the HubSpot rocket ship as it grew revenue from tens to hundreds of millions per year. Combined with interviews with accomplished sales executives and lessons learned from books and training, Signorelli builds on decades of sales expertise that will be useful for sales professionals of all levels of experience and organizational responsibility.

Having read hundreds of sales books, I have not read one that so thoroughly provides so many practical lessons."

—Peter Caputa IV, CEO, Databox

"*Inbound Selling* dismisses the notion that "sales" is a dirty word and shifts the way you think about how you sell. In departing from the well-known, pushy, and abrasive sales tactics of yesteryear, Brian advocates a highly personalized, yet scalable approach of identifying and remedying a buyer's current business challenges. He laces the pages with humorous anecdotes of humbling experiences to present an inviting learning environment for anyone in sales or anyone interested in sales. It's an evocative read that provides a turnkey framework that's as comprehensive as it is pragmatic. To put it plainly, if you're not inbound selling, you're doing it wrong."

—Rachael Plummer, sales professional
and Inbound Seller, HubSpot

"You hold in your hands a complete playbook for the journey of a sales rep from old school to what works today. Buyers have changed. Many salespeople haven't. Nearly every buying decision starts online. Buyers have as much or more information than salespeople. Salespeople need to work on improving the all-too-tenuous relationships that exist (or more likely *don't* exist) between buyers and sellers today. Sales rep processes have been shaken up due to the disruption of technology. Brian's been there and done that. He states, "I was never supposed to be in sales." Yet he learned and grew as a young rep at HubSpot into a sales leader. He's been down and dirty in the front lines of sales. He's emerged with this book and both strategic and tactical advice for how to navigate the sales journey with today's empowered buyers. Beginning with his journey as an inexperienced rep with lots of ideas, but no real sales experience, Brian walks us step-by-step through his sales journey: his emotions on hearing no over and over (and what it felt like to hear yes), his real-world experiences and how he could have done better, why he decided to move into sales management—and what he wished he had known before making that move. Unlike high-level strategic sales leadership books, which are great in theory but aren't practical in reality, this one is deep in the trenches, sharing hard-won insights from personal experience and digging into the mechanics of how to sell now. Today, not 10 years ago. Buckle up for this inbound sales journey—it's packed with actionable examples throughout."

—Lindsay Kelley,
head of digital and content marketing, Telit

"For any salesperson, sales manager, or business owner looking to learn how to adapt to the new way customers buy and turbocharge their growth, this is the book!"

—Matthew Cook, CEO, SalesHub

"The world of sales has been flipped on its axis over the past decade. Buyers have seized control from what once was a highly orchestrated, controlled, and (some would say) manipulative process. Salespeople and sales organizations have had to learn new skills and to develop new processes. A result of this "sales revolution" has been a new approach to selling called Inbound Sales. There are few people in the world who have studied, practiced, and refined the process like Brian Signorelli. In this book, Brian shares everything you need to know to be successful with this approach. It's a must-have for any salesperson or growth executive's bookshelf (or Kindle)."

—Doug Davidoff, CEO and founder,
Imagine Business Development

INBOUND
SELLING

INBOUND

SELLING

How to Change the Way You Sell
to Match How People Buy

BRIAN SIGNORELLI

WILEY

Published by John Wiley & Sons, Inc., Hoboken, New Jersey.

Published simultaneously in Canada.

For general information about our other products and services, please contact our Customer Care Department within the United States at (800) 762-2974, outside the United States at (317) 572-3993 or fax (317) 572-4002.

Wiley publishes in a variety of print and electronic formats and by print-on-demand. Some material included with standard print versions of this book may not be included in e-books or in print-on-demand. If this book refers to media such as a CD or DVD that is not included in the version you purchased, you may download this material at http://booksupport.wiley.com. For more information about Wiley products, visit www.wiley .com.

Library of Congress Cataloging-in-Publication Data
Names: Signorelli, Brian, author.
Title: Inbound selling : how to change the way you sell to match how people
    buy / Brian Signorelli.
Description: Hoboken : Wiley, 2018. | Includes bibliographical references and
    index. |
Identifiers: LCCN 2017056770 (print) | LCCN 2017058103 (ebook) | ISBN
    9781119473442 (pdf) | ISBN 9781119473275 (epub) | ISBN 9781119473411
    (hardback)
Subjects: LCSH: Selling. | Telemarketing. | Customer relations. | BISAC:
    BUSINESS & ECONOMICS / Sales & Selling. | BUSINESS & ECONOMICS / Marketing
    / Telemarketing.
Classification: LCC HF5438.25 (ebook) | LCC HF5438.25 .S567 2018 (print) |
    DDC 658.85–dc23
LC record available at https://lccn.loc.gov/2017056770

Printed in the United States of America

10 9 8 7 6 5 4 3 2 1

To Pete and Dannie

Contents

Acknowledgments

Thank you to Ryan Ball, Sam Belt, Kipp Bodnar, Dani Buckley, Peter Caputa, Matthew Cook, Doug Davidoff, Katharine Derum, Matt Dixon, Nathaniel Eberle, Debbie Farese, Jill Fratianne, Brian Halligan, Danielle Herzberg, Justin Hiatt, Lauren Hintz, Lindsay Kelley, Hunter Madeley, David McNeil, Rachael Plummer, Mark Roberge, Dan Tyre, Derek Wyszynski, Leah, Dixie, and Charlotte for contributing to this work in many ways, shapes, and forms. Thank you to my entire HubSpot family, and, of course, the team at John Wiley & Sons, for making this possible.

Foreword

I couldn't ask for a more dynamic, experienced, and exciting duo to write the foreword for this book. The sixth employee and current director of sales at HubSpot, Dan Tyre is a world-renowned speaker, adviser, mentor, and investor to companies and individuals around the world on the topic of sales. Mark Roberge was HubSpot's fourth employee and head of sales through its run up to $100 million in revenue. Now a senior lecturer at Harvard Business School, Mark served as HubSpot's SVP of Global Sales and Chief Revenue Officer from 2007 to 2016. He is the author of the best-selling book The Sales Acceleration Formula.

I've asked Dan and Mark to discuss—in their own words—the history, current state, and future of sales.

On the History of Sales through the Salesperson's Eyes
BY DAN TYRE

From my earliest recollection, the sales profession has suffered from a tarnished image. It's hard to pinpoint exactly where this reputation started. In the late nineteenth century—the early days of the geographic expansion of the United States—settlers purchased essential goods from a peddler or traveling salesman basically because they had no choice. The sales profession wasn't so much a profession as it was just someone with a horse and wagon. Transportation was the differentiating factor; the product and quality were secondary. Faced with an option to sell to a customer once and likely never see the prospect again, you can guess how that turned out. Exactly. Unfortunately, this activity usually resulted in an awful customer experience, tarnishing the image of the salesperson.

As the early US economy matured, storefronts became a more acceptable place to purchase goods and salespeople or shop owners became a bit more accommodating. It was much more important to sell and support quality products alongside good service when your customers knew who you were, how to get to your house, and saw you every day.

Fast-forward to the 1950s. The inevitable changes in mass media and technology created the Golden Age of Marketing when the *Mad Men* era gave rise to a mass marketing of products and services to a wide population, mostly through radio and TV. At that time, marketing became *more* important than sales as a way to create demand, but most salesmen (mostly a male-dominated industry at this point) maintained relatively low or nonexistent ethical, honesty, and quality levels.

MY OWN START IN SALES: THE DAYS OF THE DISENFRANCHISED BUYER

When I started my sales career as a teenager in the 1970s, the sales occupation was decidedly dicey. Sales was the land for misfit toys, a vocation of last resort, and the place managers stuck people who had very little aptitude (and in some cases, intelligence). The sales role required a lot of hard work, but it did pay well, and in most cases, you didn't have to sit in an office all day working on spreadsheets or study and pass any difficult certifications. With a grade point average that made my parents wince, I thought it might be a reasonable way to make a living for myself.

My first sales job was selling dictionaries for the Southwestern Corporation in 1976 and 1977. It was a comprehensive education in people, process, human motivation, and hard work. I went to school in Upstate New York, but was assigned a territory in Bellingham, Washington, and Portland, Oregon.

I was given no salary, one week of group sales training, and dropped off with two other sales recruits, 3,000 miles from home. Our bible at the time was Tommy Hopkins's *How to Master the Art of Selling.* The odds of success were steep. But I realized a few things that proved to be valuable lessons throughout my business career. First, people were very different and had very different reasons for purchasing a product, so a successful salesperson needed to modify behavior to increase the potential to close a deal. Second, there was an actual process to work through a sale—a similar, repeatable way that you could determine who to spend your time with and how to treat the prospect at every stage. And, third, the more times you repeated this predefined sales process, the greater your success.

In those days, we followed a very seller-centric sales process. We were indiscriminate in our approach and would sell to virtually anyone (although people with school-age children or grandkids were more qualified). Prospecting was an actual *physical* process, where you would knock on as many doors as possible to try to connect face to face (sometimes referred to as "belly to belly") with people. This process included identifying prospects, doing a small bit of qualifying to determine fit, demoing a product, leaning hard into an emotional reason to buy, answering objections, and then going for the close.

Back then, we used sales techniques like the puppy dog close (let them hold the dictionaries so they wouldn't give them back) or the porcupine close (answering a question with a question). It was fascinating to learn these skills because the sales profession was shrouded in mystery and understanding how people made decisions regarding a product purchase gave you additional power and insight into human behavior that could be applied to other parts of your life.

In the 1980s, I went to work for a startup that sold IBM personal computers and learned an evolved way of selling—solution-oriented selling. Although this was still seller centric, it involved asking a series of questions to understand the problems a prospect wanted to solve and digging into her specific information and situation to provide a unique solution. It was transformative for several reasons: First, it involved discovery of what the customer was looking for rather than the product features you were selling. Second, it required you to know something about your prospect's business and how your product would fit into that business. And, third, it became a competitive advantage for building trust and closing the deal. It worked, and it worked well.

SALES AT THE BEGINNING OF CONTENT MARKETING

For the first 25 years of my sales career, sales and marketing were diametrically opposed and almost always at odds. When you were running a company, and wanted to increase revenue, you would hire a hard-charging sales leader to come in and hire field salespeople to gain market share. In most cases, the more salespeople you added, the more revenue you generated. Marketing, however, was always in the doghouse with everyone. At the board of directors level, marketing was always an expense with little correlation to success. At the senior management level, marketing was "squishy" and hard to measure. In the trenches, marketing was always in the doghouse because they would create the brand and generate leads, but the leads were either not coming fast enough (therefore, they were in the doghouse) or exhibited questionable quality (so they were in trouble with that, too).

As virtually the entire world shifted its buying behavior online as opposed to in-person channels (2000–2010), marketing proved to be a much more important contributor to revenue generation for several reasons. First, the sheer efficiency for lead generation through a website dwarfed any type of manual lead generation process that a salesperson (or marketing department could produce). Second, the effectiveness and ease through which sellers connected with qualified buyers increased because a salesperson understood who was interested in their company's products or services. Third, inbound marketing eliminated the most time-consuming, low-value activity in the sales process (prospecting) and replaced it with a self-selection process to connect with higher value clients. Fourth, that enhanced sales process typically led to better results. Fifth, because of the online nature of the transaction, it could be accomplished via the web or phone, greatly reducing the typically high cost of most sales processes. Finally, with that high volume of transactions came an ability to capture valuable data and use it to improve the sale process itself.

In 2007, as the second salesperson for HubSpot, I was lucky enough to work with Mark Roberge and witness the dawn of the inbound marketing era. I initially cold-called to generate new business. I started with all my friends and family and connected with anyone who would listen and explained the HubSpot inbound marketing value proposition. People typically had two questions: What is inbound marketing? And, Will it work? I always smiled and explained that the discipline was new, but that it seemed to make sense to me and that I had experienced the value myself as an early HubSpot customer.

Moving from traditional sales to inbound sales was extraordinarily transformational. I went from meeting face to face at the prospect's office to meeting over the phone. I went from investing a lot of time and effort prospecting to working with people who were already expressing interest in my company's research, blog posts, and other content. I went from pushing a "pitch" to simply starting a conversation, armed with an understanding of what the prospect was likely looking for help with. Inbound was completely different because it was prospect centric, *not* seller centric. It was efficient, consultative, and just felt right.

Over the next 10 years, salespeople will have the same opportunities that marketers have had for differentiating their value based on the way in which they sell. Marketers who invested in inbound in the last decade largely saw a significant return on that investment. It will be the same for salespeople. In my opinion, it might be a bit harder for salespeople to change to the new way of doing things, but that does not make it a meaningless or worthless endeavor. In fact, quite the opposite is true.

The future is super exciting for the salesperson who is willing to learn this new way of selling, leverage the technology right in front of them, and ultimately transform the way they sell to match how people want to buy.

On the Current State of Sales and What the Decades Ahead May Hold
BY MARK ROBERGE

When I interviewed and hired the author of this book back in 2012, I had no idea of the impact he would have on our company. Accelerating through the ranks, first as a top-performing salesperson, then sales leader, Brian exhibited a form of salesperson-ship that made me proud. Seeing him assemble this work and further the entire field takes pride to an entirely new level.

In 2007, I teamed up with a few classmates from MIT to help start HubSpot, a software company based in Cambridge, Massachusetts. I was the fourth employee and first salesperson. Using many of the concepts Brian has captured in this book, I successfully scaled sales to more than 10,000 customers, generating more than $100 million in annualized revenue, and oversaw a global team of more than 400 employees. It was an amazing ride. The pace was exhilarating. The impact we had on our customers' lives was enormously gratifying. However, hiring people like Brian, watching them develop in our organization, and now seeing the broader impact they are having on the field is probably the most satisfying aspect of the experience.

Since I left HubSpot, my perspective has expanded across a range of go-to-market contexts. I teach sales and entrepreneurship full time at Harvard Business School. I help large companies transform their go-to-market functions as a senior adviser for Boston Consulting Group. I help dozens of startups each year accelerate their revenue growth as an investor, adviser, and board member. Through these experiences, I have developed an appreciation around how broad the applications of inbound selling truly are.

THE INTERNET-EMPOWERED BUYER MADE LEGACY SELLING INEFFECTIVE

As Dan noted, before the Internet, buyers had to talk to salespeople to make a purchase. They needed to understand the details of the offering, how the offering differed from the competition, how much it cost, the resources needed to install or use it, and so on. Some salespeople abused this information power. They used it to engage with buyers that were not a good fit. They manipulated the truth to get a sale. And they got away with it. Sales left a bad taste in many buyers' mouths.

The Internet changed both situations. Buyers no longer need salespeople to make purchases. Online, buyers can read about the details of the offering, compare offerings across competitors, and usually understand how much it costs. Sometimes they can even try the product and often they can buy it, all without talking to a salesperson. Does that mean sales is dead? No, in my humble opinion. However, this context shift dramatically changes the way sales must be executed.

Second, salespeople can no longer get away with jamming bad-fit products or services into buyers' hands, nor can they get away with overselling. Before the Internet, a small fraction of the addressable market would hear about this negative behavior. Today, a lot of buyers will find out and within *minutes*. Between the major social media sites like Facebook, LinkedIn, and Twitter, and customer review sites like Yelp or G2 Crowd or even niche industry forums where peers across companies are well connected, word travels fast. Overselling is the kiss a death for a salesperson, their offering, and their company.

THE TRANSFORMATION TO INBOUND SELLING

Because of these buyer context evolutions, some sales roles have been and will continue to be automated. Whether you call it "show up and throw up" or crocodile selling (big mouth, little ears), this basic form of selling will become extinct. These salespeople add no value. The information these salespeople provide is already accessible at the buyer's fingertips in a more trustworthy setting than the salesperson can provide.

For more complex selling contexts where automation is difficult, legacy salespeople will be replaced with inbound sellers. Complex contexts come in many forms. Perhaps the offering has many configurations, which makes it difficult for the buyer to understand which is best for them. Perhaps the offering is in a new, underdeveloped space and the buyer needs help understanding it. Probably most common, perhaps buyers are not sure they are framing their own business challenges or opportunities correctly. They need help from knowledgeable salespeople to understand how to frame challenges or opportunities before hearing about offerings.

In these selling contexts, inbound sellers will thrive. They will engage with buyers in a highly personalized way, turning the data accessibility of the Internet into an ally rather than an enemy. They will build trust with buyers and use that trust to understand deep buyer context. They will educate the buyer to help them frame their context even more accurately. They will present their offerings in a manner customized to the buyer's context, acting as a translator between the generic messaging available online and the unique buyer needs. These sellers will develop a reputational track record, both online and offline, that will fuel their sales success exponentially.

So, as a Seller, What Can You Do to Align with the New Selling Paradigm?

Walk in your buyer's shoes. It is not enough to understand your offering. Understanding your buyer's context is just as important. At HubSpot, every salesperson went through a month of training before they ever talked to a prospect. While they did receive some sales training, most of the training revolved around walking in the buyer's shoes. Each salesperson had to create a website and blog, publish articles, engage in social media, set up landing pages, develop email and lead nurturing campaigns, and analyze their marketing results, all using the HubSpot software. Salespeople developed a deep understanding of a marketer's challenges, related to these prospects more intimately, and could better help prospects through the challenges they were facing.

Contribute to the knowledge your buyer consumes. The best HubSpot salespeople invested time each week in engaging online where our prospects were congregating. They read the blogs the prospects read and commented on them. They followed the influencers our prospects followed and highlighted the best articles. They participated in the industry forums where prospects were active. Most impactful, they wrote guest posts on our company blog. Sometimes these efforts generated leads for the salesperson. However, more importantly, these efforts enabled these salespeople to develop trust with their prospects. They could point prospects to work they had done or work they had promoted that aligned with prospect's unique needs. These efforts also kept these salespeople on the forefront of the industry thought leadership.

Don't oversell. Be honest. Set accurate expectations. Be trustworthy. Rebrand the field of sales. At HubSpot, we measured, compensated, and promoted salespeople not just on new revenue acquisition but also on lifetime value of their customers.

Read this book. Brian helped us figure out this new mode of selling at HubSpot. He has now eloquently codified these principles into a valuable piece of work.

Preface

I started writing this book in September 2015, right before a wedding in Gloucester, Massachusetts, for two people who had become good friends of mine in the years prior. Sitting in a hotel room by myself waiting for the ceremony to begin, I had a flash of panic come over me, totally unrelated to the night ahead—I realized that I was starting to forget some of the core principles I had learned as a sales rep at HubSpot.

At that time, it had only been a year since I became a sales manager for the team that I was previously a member of. But in that short period—focusing my efforts more on coaching, training, and recruiting for my team rather than selling day in and day out—my sales "blade" seemed to be losing its edge. During one-on-one meetings, team members who had worked with me for some time started reminding me of core selling principles that had somehow slipped my memory. So, in that moment, I started to write down everything I could remember about how sales worked at HubSpot. I wanted to capture everything I had learned and that had been passed on to me. At the time, I didn't know what I would do with the resulting work, but I knew that I needed to get it out of my head before it was gone for good.

In the matter of a week or two, I had about 10,000 words written . . . and still had a lot more to say. I started to realize that, despite my mentor's advice, this would end up being more than a long blog post or even an e-book. So, I kept writing. When I was done, I had produced around 50,000 words over the course of about four or five months. But it was unstructured; it didn't have a clear arc, and it felt incomplete.

While that stream of consciousness document I started producing in that hotel room was originally intended solely for the front-line sales rep (Chapters 3 to 7), it felt like it would have been a waste had I stopped there. I had learned more as a sales manager, and had also learned so much from other executives, that it felt like a worthy endeavor to include and share those learnings too, as best as I could. As you navigate through this work, keep in mind that it's broken into roughly five parts:

- **Part 1**: The "Why?" behind Inbound Sales (Chapters 1 and 2)
- **Part 2**: How to Be an Inbound Seller: A Playbook for the Front-Line Sales Rep (Chapters 3 through 7)
- **Part 3**: How to Lead Inbound Sellers: Reflections for the Front-Line Sales Manager (Chapters 8 and 9)
- **Part 4**: What Inbound Selling Means across the Executive Suite (Chapter 10)
- **Part 5**: The Future of Sales and the Sales Profession (Chapter 11)

My humble hope in sharing what I've learned, as well as my own personal story, is that front-line sales reps take away just one thing that they might want to do differently, sales managers consider just one way they can make their team members' lives better, and that leaders in the executive suite realize their business needs to change the way it sells to match how people buy if it is to succeed in the age of the empowered buyer.

Don't hesitate to share your criticism—for better or worse—by connecting with me on LinkedIn. I look forward to hearing from you, helping you, or learning from you in the future.

Introduction

It's of paramount importance to recognize business pioneers and give credit where credit is due for industry-transforming concepts. Brian Halligan is one such pioneer, and I can't think of a better way to introduce this book than by sharing my late 2015 interview with him. Alongside his co-founder, Dharmesh Shah, he founded HubSpot in 2006, setting out on a mission to transform the way the world does marketing.

It's a funny thing though, when you set out to transform a business function. Once you accomplish that goal, it's difficult to just stop at one function. So, Brian and Dharmesh went on to expand their mission in 2014 and shared their vision for creating an entirely inbound business. The next stop on their journey lay in transforming the way the world does sales, which is, of course, what this book is all about.

So that you can develop your own understanding and appreciation for how Brian sees the sales world transforming, on the next pages I reproduce the transcript of that 2015 interview. First, though, a little bit about Brian and his background.

Brian Halligan is co-founder and CEO of HubSpot. Prior to HubSpot, Brian was a venture partner at Longworth Ventures and VP of sales at Groove Networks, which was acquired by Microsoft. Previously, Brian was a senior VP of sales at PTC.

He has co-authored two books, *Marketing Lessons from the Grateful Dead*, with David Meerman Scott and Bill Walton, and *Inbound Marketing: Get Found Using Google, Social Media, and Blogs*, with Dharmesh Shah.

Brian serves on the board of directors for the Fleetmatics Group (FLTX), a global provider of fleet management solutions. He was named Ernst & Young's Entrepreneur of the Year in

2011, a Glassdoor 25 Highest Rated CEO in 2014 and 2015, an
Inc. Founders 40 in 2016, and a #2 Best CEO of 2017 by
Employees on Comparably.

Around the community, Brian's favorite charity is Camp
Harbor View, serving nearly 1,000 youths from Boston's at-risk
neighborhoods through two four-week summer camp sessions
on Long Island in the Boston Harbor.

In his spare time, Brian follows his beloved Red Sox and is a
voracious reader. He teaches a course called Designing, Developing, and Launching Successful Products in an Entrepreneurial Environment at MIT's Sloan School of Management.[1]

An Interview with Brian Halligan, CEO and Chairman, HubSpot [2]

December 2015. Edited for length and clarity.

BRIAN: Brian, I appreciate you taking the time to chat with
me. Let's start with how you got started in sales.

HALLIGAN: I started in sales in 1990, right out of school. I'll give
you my full back story. I was an engineer in college,
an electrical engineer. I did an internship during my
junior and senior year at an engineering job, and I
concluded that I just didn't like it. Always hanging
out with the sales guys, their focus was on customers and sales. So, I inevitably went to work for a
very fast-growing software company with a strong
sales culture as a secretary for a VP of sales. They
started giving me sales projects when I became
their first BDR—in today's language—and it just
went from there. That's how I got started.

BRIAN: Tell me about that job. I'm also interested to know
how you see it being different from what sales looks
like today.

HALLIGAN: I was in outside sales, and outside sales worked back then compared to today. There was no such thing as WebEx or GoToMeeting or Zoom. You spent your whole life, basically, on a plane visiting accounts. You would fly across the country and go on a bunch of sales calls in the city. It was wildly inefficient. On a trip, I had to bring a Unix work station and a giant monitor with me, which is like a hundred-pound thing to carry through airports and through everywhere. Your hands would fall off, it was so painful.

One out of every three or four times, the meetings I had scheduled would cancel at the last minute. You slept in the city with your really heavy computer. It was ridiculous when I think about it now. Back then people wanted to see you and spend time with you. People wanted to go out to dinner with you and go to the game with you.

I just think about selling today. Outside makes no sense given the cost of a telephone call, given the technology with telepresence software, webinars, and so on. To get on a plane and fly across the country now, there's at least a 30% chance you're going to have a meeting canceled. It's just crazy. I also just think people don't want to see a sales rep face to face anymore. They don't necessarily want to have dinner with that sales rep or go to the game with the sales rep. They want to go home and see their family.

It was different when I was a sales rep. Every Tuesday was "cold-call day." You'd cold-call all day to set up appointments for the rest of the week. It was the worst day of the week. But it actually worked. People would pick up the phone back then. They didn't have caller ID. There was no email. You just called them. That was the only way you got though. People needed you more. People picked up the phone more.

Second, they were more likely to call you back because there was no good way to find out what products were in the marketplace. You'd go to the library or talk to friends. You couldn't just do a search on competitive options; it was actually hard to figure that stuff out. Buyers were much more reliant on you, whereas today, the calling just doesn't work. Nobody answers the phone.

Today, buyers don't need you as much as they used to because all that information is right at their fingertips. They can make a recording and ask questions, go to a website and find products and pricing, Google and find your competitors, connect with you on LinkedIn. It's totally different. The thing that is frustrating to me, and the thing I think is a big opportunity, is most salespeople still operate like it's 1990. It's a big opportunity, if you completely rethink it.

BRIAN: If the way the buyers buy has changed, why do you think sellers haven't caught up to that yet? Where's the disconnect?

HALLIGAN: I think behavior is hard to change. Let's say you're a sales rep and you've spent the past 20 years doing something to make your numbers. You've got a system and a process that you've developed and you're making decent money. It's just hard to change behavior. Even though intellectually it's sort of not, it makes sense. For example, you're sitting there and you're a sales rep. Calls are coming into your phone. You're looking at your caller ID, you don't answer it. You get cold emails coming in and you never answer them. You consider those cold calls when they come to you, and you consider those messages spam when they come to your email. But for some reason, in your eyes, they're *not* spam when you're sending those same emails to prospects, you call that email marketing. And it's not a cold call when you pick up the phone to call some, it's prospecting. It takes a long time for that disconnect to work its way out.

BRIAN: What's the tipping point then? Is it just waiting for a new generation?

HALLIGAN: We're seeing it on the marketing side. It's the same thing with marketers. They're still doing tons of TV ads. They're wasting their money on that. Tons of them are buying lists and spamming people. Many are doing all that old-school stuff that doesn't work as well anymore and is incredibly hard to measure. It just takes time to get past it. It's just like anything else. It just takes time for a market to adapt to modern realities.

BRIAN: One thing I've been thinking about recently is whether or not the term "inbound selling" is an oxymoron. Inbound selling is predicated on the idea of engaging prospects by listening for buying signs, answering the questions they have, and helping them solve their challenges and problems. But it still typically requires the sales rep to initiate contact, which would be considered "outbound"; the buyer didn't actually start the conversation with the rep specifically. Can a salesperson truly be *inbound*? Is it possible?

HALLIGAN: I think you can. Let's just compare and contrast how I might do it. The traditional way of doing it as a salesperson is this: I go get a list of a hundred people in my territory and I get the email addresses. The emails get sent to the company and I begin there. I'm a climber. I get the first name and the person right on the email but basically I just pound out the work. The likelihood of getting a response is so low, you might get one response. I think you're better off spending the time to call on the people who are already on your website, because you already have people you're trying to connect with on your site in the first place.

How do you call on those people on your website who have already expressed interest? How do you evaluate what they've done in your website, and then custom-tailor a perfect message to them that hits the nail on the head and pulls them back into you? The prioritization is different, calling the people who have raised their hand. The level of research is very different. Is it worth the time to do the research? I'd argue it is because people are unforgiving when it comes to poorly written, or poorly researched, email messages. They don't open them, or worse, they publicly shame you on LinkedIn. They're just completely immune to them. The question sellers must ask themselves today is: How do you create content through your email or through your call, that's just so compelling based on everything you learn about them, that they cannot resist the idea of calling you back and learning from you?

BRIAN: One point of pushback I frequently experienced when I was selling was people would say, "Hey,

Brian. Look. I get this inbound marketing thing. I love it, in fact. We want to do it. But in the next three months, while I'm getting that engine up and running, I can't wait to deliver results to the organization. I have to buy the lists. I have to do something in the meantime." I guess my question to you is: Is website traffic, using technologies to find out what companies are on your website, for example, is that sufficient for a sales team to show results?

HALLIGAN: Even if it's not, let's just say your territory is Northern California. Rather than buying a list of tech CEOs in the area and sending them the same message, you can use technology today to really understand them before you send a message, and then send them a really *good* message, or a series of messages, and an email workflow. Monitor when they open and engage with your content and messages, and then engage them in very powerful ways by pulling them back into you, even if they haven't been on your website. I get 15 cold messages a day by email or by phone. They are never customized or personalized in a way that's really compelling to me. They never refer to a recent tweet I've had, or a recent article about me in the press. They're cold. Completely cold. And so, they get no response.

BRIAN: If they did have that customization, what percentage of lift do you think you'd see? Would you respond to, say, 10% more?

HALLIGAN: If someone sent me a good email with something useful in it, I'd totally respond. I wouldn't think of them as a sales rep. I would think of how they're helping me. How do they help me as opposed to how they're selling their product? It's sort of like solution selling on steroids.

BRIAN: Okay. In terms of cross industry adoption and cross industry applicability, we get this comment a lot on the marketing side of things. "I think that inbound marketing works well for certain industries, but in this industry, not so well." I would obviously disagree with that notion, but why do you think that is?

HALLIGAN: It's an excuse not to change.

BRIAN: You think that's it? You think it's that people just don't want to change? They think, "Hey. That's great. We have a really specialized industry." Which then we would usually say something like, "Look, I understand that you're unique just like everyone else. The reality is you're not unique." Do you think there's kind of a path dependency on things that worked in the past?

HALLIGAN: Yes. Just think about email. When we first started email marketing 10 years ago, everyone thought we were freaking crazy. They were like, "What are you talking about? Social media and marketing? What? SEO? What?" I think depending on the industry, the mindset has changed. Like when we were first starting HubSpot there were very few people on Facebook. The idea of doing marketing through Facebook was a little odd to most people. Today, that's no longer an excuse. Everyone's on Facebook.

There are very few industries where I don't think inbound marketing or inbound sales is a good fit. The reality is, humans are radically changing the way they live. And the way they shop and the way they buy has changed. Without marketing and sales adapting to that change, we're going to be stuck in the past. The Internet changes everything. If you look at the Fortune 500 in 1985, of the 500 companies in the Fortune 500 in 1985, and you shift to 1995, it's like 420 or something of those companies are still on there. Once you were on the top, you stayed on top, but that's not the case today. If you look from 2005 to 2015, it's radically different.

The Internet has disrupted pretty much every industry you can think of. If you're stuck marketing and selling the old way, guess what; you're going to get disrupted. We're going through a transition now in the economy that's uncanny to the industrial revolution that happened in the 1800s. I think we're lucky we're living through such a massive shift.

To think that sales hasn't changed and to think that tricks of the trade that you did 20 years ago are going to work today to me is blasphemous.

I just think of the way people buy and the way people used to engage me as a sales rep. They needed me from the "top of the phone" to the "bottom of the mountain." Everything they wanted, I had. Today they don't need me anymore. They've got it all. They need me at the end of the transaction. And even now, more and more transactions are going touchless, so they won't even need a sales rep to do that either.

When the Internet first came along, it was very cheap to set the bottom line. eBay, Amazon. That line has moved up. The sales role has changed. The salesperson has got to be more of a consultant. The sales rep gets involved much later in the process.

BRIAN: Are there industries that are still going to require— or perhaps always require—outside sales reps? Again, does that come back to your hypothesis that people are just really, really resistant to change?

HALLIGAN: Inside, outside, I don't think that's as big a deal, whether you're selling inside or outside. I think the big change is more on the buyer's side where they've changed so much. Where access to information is wildly better than it ever was. Before, they needed to talk to you a lot. The leverage you have as a sales rep is dramatically lower now. More and more research is done on the buyer's time, not on the sales reps' time. The convincing is done all on their own now, not with sales.

I think "inside versus outside," that's not my big pet rock to shift. I certainly think that's happening, but there's a whole shift in the spectrum. It used to be that nothing was bought online. A little bit was done inside, but most everything was done outside. The whole thing's shifting to inside now.

BRIAN: What sort of evolution are we going to see in the sales world over the next 10 or 20 years?

HALLIGAN: The way it works today is: see button, click button, see a form, fill out a form, then you get a piece of content, then you'll get called by a sales rep a day later. The next step in that is you press the button, that same thing turns into, "We already know a lot about you. Schedule an appointment with the rep right now." And you get right into the rep's schedule right there. A step beyond that is, just talk to a rep right now. It's totally like when the Inbound Call Coordinator (ICC) team uses a pop up, just talk to someone now and flip the concept of waiting to speak to a salesperson on its head. I think that evolution is coming in the next year or two [at time of publication, HubSpot had realized both of these visions through its Meetings and Messages products, which are apps inside of its Sales Hub].

The other evolution that's going to happen will take a little longer as Generation Z grows up. They don't have email. They don't really use the web. They just use mobile apps. They don't really use the phone to talk. There's a paradigm shift coming there where you've got to figure out how to market to people who are completely immune to telephone calls, completely immune to email. Many don't even have email. You've got to figure out how to really market well on social media and really market well within mobile apps. That's a big shift that's going to happen in the next 10 years.

BRIAN: What do you think about the role, if any, that artificial intelligence like Watson or technologies surrounding augmented reality might play in the marketing and sales world?

HALLIGAN: Those are two very different things. I picture augmented reality more on the buyer's side, quite frankly, and the artificial intelligence more on the seller's side or on the marketer's side. I think you're going to start seeing artificial intelligence in a specific spot. Artificial intelligence is basically just where the app gets smarter and learns smarter and the personalization just gets much, much, much, much better and "guesses" better. You'll see that coming through in the next years as technology improves.

I think collaboration will get a lot better too. Look at the state of collaboration today. You've still got phones, which is kind of surprising. You have Internet calling, which isn't in full effect yet. You've got conferencing and telepresence technologies, which are all surprisingly still pretty bad. You've got Slack. That's interesting. Simple but interesting.

I just think there's a step change improvement coming over the next 10 years. You have virtual or augmented reality, I think in 5 years. The collaboration platforms will get dramatically better.

Part 1

The "Why?" behind Inbound Sales

Chapter 1

I Was Never Supposed to Be in Sales

There is simply not enough written on the topic of sales from the front-line reps' or front-line sales managers' perspective—the ones bringing billions in revenue into millions of businesses, day in and day out. They are the ones that truly understand the nature of today's buying and selling environment, and it's my opinion that theirs are the voices that matter most. And that their voices should be heard. My goal here is to give them that voice.

Of course, there are volumes upon volumes of literature written about sales management, sales leadership, sales tactics, and more. Yet, these front-line stories are being told too infrequently, mostly because the ones who write anything about sales haven't sold anything in the past decade. Beyond the obvious, that's a problem because by the time those individuals—the academic, retired professional, consultant, or sales executive—writes his or her book, the landscape has inevitably changed. They also won't tell you the truth about what really happens on the front lines of sales because they do not know anymore.

Beyond that, I'm writing my story because the world of sales has changed! *Drastically!* The same way that the marketing world has experienced dramatic change over the past decade, so, too, has the sales world. Many times, for example, we hear from marketers that over 60% of a buying decision is complete before a prospect ever connects with a sales rep,[1] though I'm not quite convinced that sales reps and sales professionals fully understand the magnitude and impact of that reality. They almost seem to be in denial of the fact that buyers are—unequivocally—in complete control.

Before a buyer ever speaks to a sales rep today, they have already done an immense amount of research in private or, at the very least, in the absence of a sales rep. They know your business. They know your competitors. They likely know your products' or services' strengths and weaknesses, as seen through the eyes of your customers. They may even know you. How?

The modern buyer uses a myriad of tools at their disposal, such as Google and third-party customer review sites, like G2Crowd and TrustRadius. They have already figured out where your product stands relative to those of other leaders, and they already have a sense of who your executive leadership team is. If they want to learn about anyone at your company, all they need to do is search LinkedIn.

What led to the rise of the empowered buyer? Here is an *extremely* abbreviated history: Internet magnates like Sergey Brin, Larry Page, Mark Zuckerberg, Biz Stone, Reid Hoffman, and countless others transformed the way in which we all access and synthesize information—through search and connectivity. With this newfound access to seemingly perfect, limitless, and integrated information, came a shift in how we all make buying decisions. Simultaneously, technologies also arose that enable anyone to completely block out unwanted messaging. Technologies like TiVo allow us to skip right over commercials; satellite radio empowers us to eliminate ads altogether; caller ID gives us the choice of accepting or rejecting anyone's call; and services like the National Do Not Call Registry—to an extent—put the power back in the consumers' hands, preemptively blocking telemarketers from breaking up family dinner, for example. Translation: Yesterday (pre-Google), most everyone had to rely on mediums like TV, magazines, tradeshows, newspapers, the Yellow Pages, or even cold calls from sales reps to get answers to the questions they were asking. All the control was in the hands of corporations, and their sales teams. Today, not only does the Internet allow modern buyers and consumers to take back that control, empowering them to find information they need on their own terms, it turns out that people enjoy this self-led experience far better than being interrupted. So, the power has shifted away from corporations and traditional media platforms, and back into the modern buyer's hands.

While the challenges that came with this democratized access to information are well known in the global marketing community, they seem, in a way, to have been lost on their sales counterparts. Where does all this change in the way that people find, or block, information leave the modern sales rep? In a phrase: *Gone are the days where buyers rely on sales reps for information.* Therefore, as sales professionals, we need to change the way we sell to better match the way that the world now consumes information and makes its buying decisions. We must do this without having nearly the amount of control or, in fact, any control that reps of yesterday may have enjoyed. We must evolve and find new, relevant ways to connect with, and engage, buyers. Simply creating a target account list and cold-calling straight through it, repetitively, is dead.

Here are some facts that help shed light on how challenging today's selling environment is for sellers:

- ♦ Over 60% of the sales decision-making process is done before the sale is made (CEB Research).[2]
- ♦ By 2020, it is expected that as much as 80% of a buying decision will be done *without* a sales rep (Forrester).[3]

- Once a rep gets to the sales conversation, more than 50% of the decision-making process is driven not by *what* they sell, but *how* they sell (*Challenger Sale*).[4]
- Over 90% of CEOs said they *never* respond to cold emails or calls. For the ones that do, only 2% of all outreach turns into a meeting scheduled (*Forbes*).[5]

One of my hopes in writing this story is to do nothing more than share what I've learned, felt, and experienced with anyone who should feel so inclined to keep reading. At no point in this story will I claim to be a de facto expert. I've simply learned an immense amount through experience and expect to only learn volumes upon volumes more as I continue my career in sales. But I think it's critical to share what I've learned so far, document it, and make the front-line sales rep's and manager's perspective widely available.

I started my career as a research analyst a decade ago (about 2007), jumped into the startup world for a few years after that, and then decided to take the plunge into the sales world. No experience, no training, no prior coaching or knowledge. All I had was my mixed bag of experiences across five years and a determination to give sales a shot for at least one year.

So, my desires above all else in sharing this story are to:

1. Inspire sales reps and sales leaders to rapidly adapt to the new sales world reality, so that they may thrive.
2. Encourage reps yet to be born, considering a career switch into sales, considering a switch out of sales, or somewhere along their sales journey to keep going and take only the bits and pieces of this story that work for them.
3. Create the possibility to improve the all-too-tenuous relationships that exist between buyers and sellers today.

To understand where we're going together, I'd like to take you with me to the beginning of my own story. It isn't necessarily interesting, and it probably isn't unique. But it's my story, and I think it's worth sharing with you, if for no other reason than context for how I arrived at where I am today.

When I came to HubSpot in 2012, I had no idea what I was getting myself into. I had no sales experience, no training, and I had never been fully involved in a sales "process," I had never really asked anyone for money, at least not in the sales sense. What I did have, however, was a desire to make money, or at least that's how I perceived my sense of motivation in life back then (I would later come to find this was only partially true, and mostly derived from the fact that I'd been living paycheck to paycheck for the prior five years). I'm not sure where that desire came from, but it has been present my entire life. Rest assured, however, that this fascination is not what you think. I never did, nor do I now, value money for the sake of money. It's the freedom that it represents, and the work almost always required to get it, that motivates me the most.

A brief timeline of events that led up to my adventure in sales at HubSpot: By the time I graduated from college (circa 2007) and secured my first job, I literally had $100 to my name. And that Benjamin Franklin needed to last me approximately two weeks until my first paycheck hit my meager checking account. The time passed, the check came, and I made it.

More time went on and I couldn't manage to save all that much. Even when I got my first bonus for a whopping $2,500 (which I thought was a ton of money until someone explained how corporate bonuses were taxed), it was barely enough to keep me on schedule paying rent. I never really worried about running out of money that much, I just had this deep desire to never need to think about it—to be able to buy what I wanted, when I wanted, whenever I wanted. I never wanted to have to check my bank account before buying something.

If I were to strictly adhere to a chronological regurgitation of events, I would go into my work experience at the Corporate Executive Board (CEB, acquired by Gartner in 2017[6]). However, I won't go into much detail because this is supposed to be a book about my transition into and experience with sales so I'll keep the focus there. But there were a couple of important seeds planted in my head while I was at CEB—from 2007 to 2010—that I think are relevant and worth sharing.

The first seed planted came about two years into my time at CEB, when I sat in on my first sales call. I can't remember the sales rep's name, I just remember that he was "smooth." Very smooth. Too damn smooth! What struck me as odd, however, was the way in which he opened that call I joined back then. It went something like this:

> *Hi [Prospect Name]—Thanks so much for taking some time to chat with us.* [He went on to make introductions after that]. *Tell me, Mr. Prospect, what do you know about Corporate Executive Board?*

It struck me as odd. Was this how all sales calls opened? Was it a sales tactic? I don't remember how the rest of the call continued, but that opening line really stuck with me. It just seemed so unnatural and off-putting. Wasn't the sales rep supposed to be learning about the prospect's business and that individual's role first, instead of the other way around?

The second seed planted in my mind came about six months after that experience. I was helping the company grow a line of business in the federal government space. I was responsible for organizing the team, contributing to the corporate strategy, driving our underpinning marketing efforts, as well as writing responses for applications to get us on the General Services Administration and contracting schedules for the Library of Congress. And when I say "I was responsible for," I mean, "I was the grunt who did the heavy lifting at the discretion of a Managing Director." As I helped this business get off the ground, I saw a lot of salespeople around me making a *lot* of money. Eventually, we needed to fill a spot on the sales team, and I briefly flirted with the idea of making the leap to sales then. I don't specifically recall why I decided against it—perhaps there was too much risk—or perhaps I already had one foot out the door. Either way, I didn't take the role and continued to crank away as a research analyst for about another seven months.

In retrospect, I believe these two seeds—observing sales firsthand (and frankly, being somewhat flabbergasted at what I saw) and flirting with the idea of getting into sales—set me on a path to at least consider the sales profession in the future. I was fascinated by how sales reps approached conversations. I was even more amazed at how they could start a conversation with something that sounded as arrogant as "What do you know about us?" and somehow end it with a prospect signing a contract for tens of thousands if not hundreds of thousands of dollars. Compounding this fascination, as a research analyst at the time, I truly believed *I* was the one creating all the value and getting paid for a small fraction of the results. This, I knew, was a great injustice! So, as the age-old saying goes, "If you can't beat 'em, join 'em." I eventually did.

In mid-2010, I decided to make what felt like a big career switch and go to a startup because I was offered an *amazing* amount of equity: a whopping 20% stake in the company! By the way, if you didn't catch my attempt at sarcasm, 20% of nothing is . . . nothing. Of course, that alone wouldn't suffice if I were to truly escape the corporate world and live the bohemian startup life, so I gladly *also* took a $30,000 pay cut in the process.

I was brought on to run sales and marketing for a tiny little business you've probably never heard of called GiftsOnTime. Obviously, this was a perfect fit for my set of skills as a research analyst, considering I spent absolutely zero time doing any sales or marketing at CEB and had exactly zero education in either discipline. Reflecting on it, I think I tried to express how real my lack of experience was to my business-partners-to-be, but I'm sure they countersold into my ego. Replaying this conversation in my mind's eye, it sounded something like this (paraphrased):

> *Siggy, you're a smart guy and a hard worker. It doesn't matter that you haven't done any of this. We haven't either. You'll figure it out as you go. We're all in it together, anyway.*

I took the bait . . . hook, line, and sinker. I-d-i-o-t.

So, starting in September 2010, I took the sales and marketing reins at GiftsOnTime and had to address a few pressing issues. First, our vendor relationships were totally screwed up. We were relying on two vendors and needed to reduce our exposure to relying on just those two for all our product fulfillment. So, we took care of that by building marketing materials and cold-calling into companies like Brookstone, 1-800-Flowers, Godiva, and Tiffany's. Looking back on it, in some ways I was shocked that I sold them on allowing us to resell their products on our site. We were absolute nobodies! We didn't even have one paying customer at the time.

Once we took care of that little issue (which I assure you was not little, and did in fact continue to be an issue that we should have taken more seriously), I moved on to the next big task—getting our sales and marketing strategy in place to go to market! Hooray!

My business partners at the time had spent the previous three years building software prototype after prototype, which ultimately culminated in a beta product ready for release (sort of) around November 2010.

My God, I remember those first few months so clearly. September through the end of the year was insane. We worked seven days a week, had conference calls with everyone constantly, poured money into ads, bought every email list we could get our hands on, and shelled out seven grand every month for an agency building our social media presence.

I think we generated something in the ballpark of $20,000 to $30,000 in transactions in our first month with a "live" product, but it was also the December holidays, which is, more or less, the Super Bowl time of year for anyone in e-commerce. It was thrilling to see orders coming in—albeit mostly from friends and family. Back to the sales and marketing strategy.

As you can see in my notes about how we were initially marketing ourselves, we learned two important things: (1) We liked spending money on marketing activities that were expensive, and (2) we hated tracking the return on investment (ROI) of those efforts. So, what did we decide to do next? Trade shows! Again, knowing nothing about sales and marketing, I figured, "What better way to build a prospect pipeline than to be directly in front of our ideal buyers?!" Looking back on it, I don't completely blame my younger self for thinking this way. Intuitively, it made sense. People have been going to trade shows to do business for a long time. We also thought we were brilliant by targeting specific associations that fit our buyer profiles and personas. And it might have *actually* been genius if it weren't for three realities about most trade shows: First, they are mostly vacations for all attendees. Second, they are full of influencers, not decision-makers. Third, they're mostly brand-awareness events, not closing events.

Coming down from our trade show highs, we had "amazing" (also known as "not amazing") direct-mail and email campaigns lined up to nurture everyone we met at the trade show. We ran at that hard for the first few months of the year. It wasn't until May or June 2011—about nine months into our marketing launch efforts—that we realized it wasn't working. As in "crash and burn" not working.

Very sadly, I remember how excited we were to go to our first trade show. We had our booth built, plane tickets booked, a 400-pound trade-show box ready to be shipped to Orlando, had our pitch down, and all print marketing collateral ready. We had our armor on and felt like we were ready to sell . . . whatever selling meant.

That very first conference we went to was for the Legal Marketing Association, and the attendees appeared to be so fascinated by our business model. But that was just it . . . they were just fascinated. We won next to no business out of that trade show, but after the show ended we truly thought we were millionaires. Millionaires, I tell you! We had collected over 300 business cards. I so vividly remember sitting in our hotel room, looking at all those business cards, each of us with a drink in hand and sore feet from standing for three days straight. I said, "So, this is what a million dollars looks like."

I was so naïve, but I thought I was so brilliant in the moment. I thought that was *our* moment. The exact moment in time into which all our hard work culminated. That pinnacle moment that we just knew we were going to make it.

When we followed through after that conference we saw some positive feedback but nothing substantial. We had a handful of other conferences lined up for human resources professionals, real estate professionals, accountants, financial services providers, and more. We had our trade show circuit and plan down pat. Yet in the end, we had nothing to show for it. Then, somewhere along the way—in the throes of giving birth to that business—everything changed. I found HubSpot.

Truth be told, I didn't find HubSpot; HubSpot sort of found me. When I was working at GiftsOnTime we were working with two technology consultants that were helping us outsource our software development—I'll call them Roger and Barry. At one point along the way, Barry jumped in and helped me dissect our sales and marketing plan. He thought it was crazy for us to be paying a marketing agency $7,000 a month (which it was, for this particular agency) and to be buying every technology under the sun, never mind spending hundreds of thousands of dollars on trade shows that we thought were putting us in front of our target audience. He was right, but it was an incredibly humbling and embarrassing moment for me privately. Barry pointed me in the direction of Verndale—a local technology and marketing consulting firm. He also pointed me in the direction of a small startup technology company at the time called HubSpot. When I compared the price for each side by side—about $100,000 a year (Verndale) versus $10,000 a year (HubSpot)—I was obviously attracted to the latter for the very stupid but very valid reason that we had spent so much money on sales and marketing tactics that failed us previously. We were literally down to the last $10,000 to $20,000 of what was once a sizable sales and marketing budget. We had no choice.

My HubSpot sales reps were Jon Marcus (serial entrepreneur) and Mike Redbord (now VP and GM of the Customer Hub for HubSpot). I remember that first conversation we had so vividly.

Jon: "So, what do you guys do?"

Brian: "Well, we're kind of a software company and kind of an ecommerce company. We have a software platform that allows our customers to automate all their business gift-giving throughout the year. It's designed for accountants, attorneys, financial advisers, real estate agents, etc. Anyone who maintains a client relationship and uses gift-giving as an ongoing marketing and customer retention tool could benefit from our service and software."

Jon: "Okay, so how do you make money?"

Brian: "Well, we don't get paid for the software. We give the software away for free right now because we think we need to get the market to adopt the platform. There are tons of competitors out there that people are used to using, such as Godiva, Harry & David, Wine.com, and so on. So, to get people to break out of the status quo, we think we need to give the software away for free. As for making money, we take a margin on the products we sell, anywhere from 15% to 40%, depending on the product."

JON: "Okay, and how's that going for you?"

BRIAN: "Not so well."

JON: "Why do you think that is?"

BRIAN: "Well we feel like we've used every marketing tactic in the book. We have a website, have Google analytics running on the site, we have been paying an AdWords consultant, we hired a marketing agency to get us published on major websites and build our social media presence, we purchased lists to run email campaigns, we purchased technology like Constant Contact and Tableau to deliver those emails and understand our user universe, we've also done a handful of direct mail campaigns, placed ads in trade show publications, and spent over a hundred thousand dollars on trade shows themselves. We've done so much for the past year and we feel like we have so little sales to show for it."

JON: "What about your website? Do you generate any leads through your site?"

The conversation went on like this for a while. But the light really went off in my head when Jon asked the last question that I paraphrased above. You'll also notice that at no point in those first series of questions did Jon say a single thing about HubSpot; instead, he focused the entire conversation on us and our needs (go back and read the dialogue carefully to see the use of "you" and "your").

Jon helped us realize our website had been doing absolutely nothing for us. We also realized that we spent loads of time and money building a product that no one knew about and had no way to find and that this must have been our problem. And we were partially right. We were right that our website was not a lead generation tool and was not being the "sales rep" that it should be. I think we were also right that the service we were providing could create value for a significant number of people. The real problem that we had was simple: We had no idea how to run a software business.

The startup failure aside, I was truly blown away with HubSpot and using its inbound marketing methodology when we launched our first campaign through their platform. We only wrote a couple of blog posts, placed one call-to-action on our site—something like "Download the Ultimate Guide to Client Gift-Giving"—and published a landing page to convert the people interested in that blog post on our site into leads. In other words, we gave them value in the form of an e-book that educated them; we got value when they shared a little information about themselves with us to get that e-book. I realize this may sound elementary now, but in 2010 and 2011, it was a big deal.

Within the very first day of publishing those blog posts, that call-to-action (which, by the way was buried in our homepage's footer), and the corresponding landing page, we generated over 40 new leads. Most of these leads were people we had never heard of and had never met before. It was the instant success we were searching for. Yet in that same moment of elation, I almost simultaneously panicked. I crashed from the high. I faced a new problem. What happened next? I had absolutely no idea what a sales process was, how to implement one, or how to measure the quality of execution. But I *loved* inbound marketing. It made sense to me. It was simple. And it worked. So, I metaphorically hid from this scary sales monster in my inbound marketing fort. When it came to GiftsOnTime, the inbound marketing process was simple:

- ♦ Who are you trying to attract to your website?
- ♦ What are their biggest problems, goals, or challenges?
- ♦ How would they ask someone about those problems, goals, or challenges in the form of a question?
- ♦ Turn said questions into blog articles.
- ♦ Publish those articles to your website, share them via social media, even use them in your PPC ads!
- ♦ Get more website traffic, get more leads.

Okay, it's slightly more complicated than that. But at the same time, that's pretty much it! At least, that was it to drive the site traffic. The leads, the opportunities, the customers . . . that's a bit more complex. But even that part isn't so complex so long as you continue to add value to a decision-making process over a long, or even short, period.

I pushed and pushed for the rest of that year, trying with all my might to make GiftsOnTime's revenue engine work. Sadly, and in my own opinion, at the end of 2011 we weren't generating remotely enough revenue to continue onward. We were probably seven figures in the red, and the bleeding didn't show signs of slowing. We laid off a handful of employees, others quit, and we scaled back our operation at the exact time we needed to scale up but had very limited cash to do so. We had to face the music that so many other startups face—we weren't going to make it because we ran out of money.

I decided to leave GiftsOnTime around February 2012. The split from a man I considered, and still consider to this day, my second father and my best friend from childhood was very tough. We all aged more than we wanted to because of it and learned our lessons in a way that we hoped we never would. Best intentions all around; worst outcomes.

During that time, I also received some much-needed advice from my former boss (at the Corporate Executive Board), Sampriti, who helped me take the leap of faith out of GiftsOn-Time. The same woman I had let down by skipping out on business school, in the end, was also the one that helped me turn my career around in a huge way. This is the email I wrote to her in early 2012, seeking wisdom:

Subject Line: Was wondering if you could help . . .

January 2, 2012

Hey Sampriti,

Happy New Year! Hope you and the family had a great time over the holidays. What'd you all end up doing?

I also wanted to give you an update on the business and share some of my thoughts for 2012, hoping you might be able to point me in the right direction.

To keep a long story short, GiftsOnTime didn't do well this year. There were obviously many contributing factors (some controllable, others not so much), but a lot of money has already gone into the operation with little to show in return. In other words, if I were an investor, I don't think I would be willing to go any further (given the amount of time and money that has already gone in). It's also concerning to me that we lost a significant number of "whale" accounts that we were relying on to bring us into the New Year and don't have many "deals" lined up in 2012. So, I'm starting to ask myself, "What's the deal in 2012?" Do we go back to the drawing board and stick it out for one more year, or cut the losses short and be thankful for the opportunity we had while we had it?

Ron and Josh are already fully committed to another year of running the business. I haven't talked to them about it, but I can't say that I'm feeling quite as enthusiastic or committed. And when I reflect on the past 16+ months, I feel like I've (i.e., all of us) learned a tremendous amount in new areas of business (sales, marketing, corporate communications, general management, software development, VC presentations, etc); however, I'm wondering how much "new stuff"/incremental learning there is to be had. I know that probably sounds self-centered, but it's just me being honest with myself. I guess the truth is that I don't see light at the end of this tunnel and I'm not sure how much more I have to gain by continuing down this path.

I have a few ideas in mind for opportunities in Boston that I would like to explore, but that's still a few months off. So, before I get any further ahead of myself, I thought I would ask you for your thoughts. I'm sure there's no silver bullet, but you've always seemed to get my head straight no matter how many times I've managed to crank it around the winch.

If it's easier to catch up over the phone, I'd be more than happy to do that as well.

Hope you're doing well and look forward to catching up soon.

Best,
Sig[7]

And Sampriti's response:

> *Hey Brian, happy new year to you. I hope you had a great holiday with your family. Certainly sounds like you've got a lot on your mind. It's probably better to have this conversation via phone. Until then I leave you with a thought and that is something to consider. The more fundamental question I have in addition to what you are likely to learn this coming year is what assumptions need to change in order for the business to be successful? If you aren't sure what those assumptions are, nor do you believe they are likely to change, then I would suggest it may be time for you to evaluate other options.*
>
> *Another thing to consider is if you're not in for another year the way your business partners are, is it fair to just commit partway?*
>
> *Let me know when you would like to speak next week and we can flesh out how best to proceed.*
>
> *Regards,*
> *Sampriti* [8]

It was then that I knew, when I read, *"if you're not in for another year the way your business partners are, is it fair to just commit partway?"*

I knew in my gut that the answer was "No." And I knew that it was a hard no because it was the same decision-making process I had gone through when I decided to leave Sampriti only about two years prior. I was out. I knew I was out, and once you realize that, you should leave. There is no way to be successful or to be fulfilled if what you're doing does not bring you fulfillment. If you are not inspired or motivated by what you are doing, or the work your company is doing, it will ultimately show up in your work. Once it shows up, you're cooked. It's best to get out early and leave on a high note than to drag yourself—and those around you—down in the process only to collect a few extra paychecks. It was then that I decided to make my move and start pursuing new opportunities. But what would I pursue? I had such a strange medley of experience. I had no idea where I might add value to another company.

Reflecting on my experience as a HubSpot customer, I felt like I would be an excellent customer onboarding specialist. I knew the product well, lived the pain the company solved for, and felt analytical enough to become a master educator on both the inbound methodology and the software. However, as I began the interview process, Mike (Redbord) convinced me to pursue sales instead of the inbound marketing consultant role (which is now called an Implementation Specialist).

After my experience trying to build a sales pipeline at GiftsOnTime, I wasn't exactly sold on the idea of sales at first. I had the worst impression of sales. I hated cold-calling, hated crafting outreach emails that would never get read, and loathed writing direct-mail campaigns and stuffing envelopes going to people that would just throw them in the trash. I had also been on the other side of the buying equation, and generally hated the way most sales reps tried to play games with me. They were mostly self-serving, taught me basically nothing, and went negative in a childish way when it became clear to them that I was not ready to move forward. The only time I didn't feel that way was when I went through the HubSpot sales process. I thought there might be something to that, so I spoke with my dad about the idea of pursuing sales.

The more I thought about it, the more I convinced myself that I had to work for HubSpot. The company was disruptive. It was flying in the face of conventional wisdom about how marketing worked. And I loved that. I had to be a part of it.

Ultimately, my dad convinced me to give sales a shot for a year, to give it my all, and if it worked out then to keep going. If not, I would go back into research or consulting.

This is what I refer to as my second awakening in my professional career. The first was when I became a student of inbound marketing. It had flipped all conventional knowledge I had about marketing on its head. It made sense to me, and it worked. This awakening to pursue sales as a profession—the second awakening—was even more powerful. In retrospect, it showed me that everything I thought I knew about sales was wrong and sales didn't have to be the way I had experienced it to be—in short, a thankless, dirty, low, and disrespected profession.

As I pursued this career with HubSpot further, things immediately started to feel different from as early as my first call with a recruiter. My first phone screen was with a woman named Lisa. My first manager phone screen was with Doug (now my colleague). My second phone screen was with Pete Caputa and Dannie Herzberg (who would ultimately become my manager). My in-person interviews were with Chris, John, Pete, and Dannie, and I think one more person that I can't remember. The "at home" portion of the interview process also included a two-hour, SAT-style exam laden with behavioral and analytical questions. I was also required to do a mock role-play as a part of the process before my in-person, final round of interviews.

Simply by experiencing the intensity of the interview process, I felt reassured that I was in the right place. These people were truly challenging everything about me. They also had zero reason, whatsoever, to hire me as a sales rep. Sure, I had five years of work experience, just not in sales. I was analytical and did not consider myself outgoing. I worked for a small startup that failed. My main objectives at the startup included customer acquisition and raising investor funds, both of which I failed to achieve. The battle was uphill the whole way, but I somehow, in the end, convinced them to take a chance on me. Either that, or they were just desperate for warm bodies. Or both. I doubt they were desperate, but I still believe both forces were at play. I was never *supposed* to be in sales; yet, here I was, a job offer from HubSpot in hand. The journey was already under way.

Chapter 2

Why Inbound Sales Matters

Despite my own perception that I wasn't supposed to be in sales, here I am! Approaching a decade now and going strong. For any tenured sales professional reading my story, you may be chuckling to yourself, thinking, "There's no way this guy knows much about sales. You can't magically replicate years and years of field experience." I won't disagree with you. You can't replicate years of field experience. Those years made you the great sales professional you've become. However, I think you'd be hard-pressed to find a sales professional today who doesn't think the job is getting harder than it has been in the past or a sales rep who doesn't think it's getting harder and harder to meaningfully connect with prospects consistently. I think you'd also struggle to find a sales rep, sales manager, or sales VP who doesn't find it even the least bit challenging to navigate through the ever-changing sales tech landscape. Last, because the new sales normal is evolving before our very eyes, no one knows exactly how it works, or will work in the future; therefore, there's no concept of someone who has "figured it out" because little has been figured out yet.

These things are true because the way people want to buy is evolving. It has fundamentally changed not only because we as people have become extremely clever in the way we block daily interruptions but also because we've also become particularly adamant about finding information on our own terms and on our own time. Just think about how you buy things yourself today. The first place you turn is probably Google or Amazon, then you might hop on LinkedIn or Facebook (depending on what you're looking for) and ask friends or professional connections for recommendations. Am I right? If you think I am, then you would also have to agree that sales professionals must evolve the way in which they sell to be considered relevant in the modern buyer's purchasing equation. What worked in the past may very well continue to work in the future, but it does not *guarantee* it will work.

In addition, while I find it imperative to study the history of sales strategy and training, I would be doing a disservice to the current sales force if I were to simply draw insights from the past and rewrap them as my gift to you on how to sell today. You likely already know a great deal about what has been done in the past and what has worked throughout the past one, two, or even three decades. You know these things because the people training you lived through those times and obtained that knowledge. At best, they are trying to take the highlights of what worked for them and pass them on to you. At worst, they are trying to pass on their mistakes in the hope you won't make them yourself.

So, instead of providing you with a chronological history of what has worked across a wide variety of firms and industries, I'm going to attempt to share with you what is *currently* happening on the front lines of sales—and what has worked for me, the reps I've worked with, and the reps I've led. Of course, all of this could become irrelevant by the time it gets into your hands, but I'm confident that won't be the case for at least a little while to come.

Moreover, my hope in sharing what I've learned in my relatively short time as a sales professional is *not* that you adopt what you're reading in its entirety. If everyone simply copies and pastes what everyone else is doing, it will become irrelevant and ineffective almost instantaneously. Instead, I hope you find the nuggets of knowledge you can adopt, adapt, and apply to your own sales process, ultimately helping you help more people, help your company grow, help you grow professionally, and build more confidence in yourself as an individual.

While I do believe that elements of the sales process and methodology I'm about to describe are widely applicable to both inside sales and field sales across the SMB, mid-market, enterprise spaces, I do think specific parts of this approach are best suited for an inside sales team; or at least the inside portion of a largely outside sales force. Additionally, because I believe that more and more companies will continue to grow their inside sales teams—as opposed to outside teams—this approach will only become more relevant as time goes on. Why do I believe this even though Forrester predicts 1 million sales jobs will be replaced by, or lost to, technology by 2020?[1] Research indicates that the inside sales role will grow at 15 times the rate of the outside sales role in the future.[2] So, while the overall volume of sales jobs may be on the decline, the need for consultative inside sales professionals will steadily rise.

Regardless of whether you're an inside sales rep now, become one in the future, plan to hire more of them, or currently lead them, you must have a baseline understanding of what a "great sales rep" looks like and what it does not. In other words, if we don't understand the archetype for the new age sales rep—which in fact is much less of a traditional, transactional rep who controls information and much more of a consultant who analyzes it, interprets it, and disseminates it—then implementing the selling framework presented in the following chapters will ultimately prove worthless to you. Not "just anyone" will do.

Core Characteristics of the Modern Sales Rep

So, what does that "new age," modern sales rep look like? Even though plenty of people would want you to believe the "real" answer is something far more complicated, to me, it comes down this. A modern sales rep:

- Leverages technology to their advantage, often to understand who to start a conversation with, when, and why
- Understands how to hold a business conversation focused on clear goals and challenges because they actually understand *who* their ideal buyer is before a conversation even starts
- Displays deep industry knowledge, because they are truly passionate about the solutions their company brings to buyers in its segment
- Demonstrates comfort discussing a variety of alternative solutions with a buyer, which often includes doing nothing, or even using a competitor's product or service
- Tailors every conversation to the buyer's specific situation, needs, and timeline
- Openly disagrees when they think a buyer's proposed solution to a goal or challenge is wrong, or that their judgment is blurred by fear, uncertainty, or doubt
- *And above all else*: The inbound seller prioritizes a buyer's needs ahead of their own

It is *that* simple. Yes, hard to teach and hard skills to find, but these behaviors are at the core of the modern seller's mindset.

Now, if you want a little more actionable advice with some examples on how to identify the true modern seller, keep in mind that past sales experience does not necessarily predict future success. Therefore, the way that we have adjusted our interviewing techniques needs to revolve around core attributes as opposed to activities—ability and cultural fit, as opposed to experience.

When HubSpot's former VP of sales, Peter Caputa (now CEO of Databox), interviews a rep, he evaluates them across four core areas deeply tied to someone's attributes, not their sales experience. He asks himself these four questions, every time, for every single candidate:

1. Does this sales rep have the desire to be successful in sales no matter what? What proof do I have?
2. Does this person have a positive outlook on the products and services he or she sells or would be selling? Why?
3. Does this person have a positive outlook on themselves? What evidence do we have to believe they have that positive outlook?
4. Do I believe that this person will take responsibility for all sales outcomes, no matter what, or will they make excuses? Why do I believe my answer to that question?

As a hiring manager, I asked myself these four core questions, but I also looked for the following in my own reps:

- Do I believe you have a high level of emotional intelligence and self-awareness? Can you put yourself in someone else's position and empathize with the challenges they're expressing? (In my opinion, this skill cannot be taught.)
- Do you have the "grinder"/"hustler" instinct and a high level of work ethic?
- Are you a lifetime achiever? Were you the kid that had the lemonade stand, the newspaper route, and the landscaping business (or any small business, for that matter)?
- Are you a strong problem solver, who can marshal a variety of internal resources to get the outcomes you need?
- To what extent are you coachable? Can you show me proof that you're coachable?
- Do you take responsibility for outcomes in life or do you make excuses?

◆ Do you possess the ability to educate and teach? Will you push back on a prospect when they reject you or challenge you?

◆ To what extent are you goal oriented? Have you set personal goals for yourself that professional achievements will allow you to pursue? What are those? How did you come up with them?

◆ And almost as important as the first question on this list, do you enjoy learning? If you do, why is that and can you show me concrete supporting examples?

Behaviors such as these are well documented in Mark Roberge's *The Sales Acceleration Formula*,[3] which should come as little or no surprise considering that Mark served as HubSpot's chief revenue officer through its run up to and through $100MM in revenue.

My only point in highlighting these frameworks is to encourage thinking about a few important things as they relate to being a successful, modern-age sales rep:

◆ As a rep, are you exhibiting these competencies and do you exude these attributes? Sales is not what it once was; it has changed intensely in the past decade. You need these skills to be successful in any organization.

◆ As a leader, are you evaluating candidates on models that aren't working, or are outdated? Are you putting too much weight on experience or attributes that do not hold up in practice? Are you putting too much experience on external accomplishments and not enough on emotional capacity and intelligence? If you're uncertain—for which you can quickly get a sense through voluntary and involuntary turnover and attainment relative to industry benchmarks—then perhaps it's time to figure out whether the evaluation model you have in place is still relevant to today's selling environment. If it isn't, it's time to rethink that model.

With these behavioral aspects of the rep built for the twenty-first century in mind, let's explore how the sales process itself has changed and what reps must do differently today to be viewed as relevant by the modern, empowered buyer.

Why Inbound Sales Matters

If I haven't already made myself abundantly clear, the way people buy from businesses has changed. Inbound sales is relevant because it teaches sellers how to change the way they sell to match the new way people want to buy. Come take a walk with me down memory lane and I'll tell you my own story about how this is playing out in the real world.

As I briefly described in the previous chapter, before I came to work at HubSpot I had the chance to observe enough sales processes to formulate an opinion on the sales profession, which, to say the least, was not favorable. While this may be slowly evolving, I am convinced most businesses still sell using outdated, underhanded tactics today. There are three specific observations that come to mind when I reflect on my experience as a buyer.

First, back then, if a sales rep got me on the phone, I was usually willing to listen to what they had to say. I took cold calls because I didn't know what I didn't know. I didn't do this all week long, but I made it part of my weekly routine. I always had a couple of minutes to talk to someone. Of course, if I was getting bombarded with calls all day, I'd start turning them down. But, in general, I was open to connecting with someone new for about 5% of my week.

Second, when I did connect, I often found if I shared even only a small insight about my business at first the sales rep would immediately latch onto that. They would *rarely* ever dig deeper to understand the meaning behind the meaning of what I just shared with them. For example, they might tell me that their business helps small businesses reach more prospects.

They would ask a question about how we were going about identifying and reaching out to prospects now, then I would answer. Shortly after that, they would immediately jump into how their product or service helped us achieve that goal more efficiently, faster, or at lower cost. They didn't dig any deeper.

Third, most reps I spoke with were incredibly focused on themselves and their own objectives. They always seemed to feel this incredible sense of urgency that I rarely ever felt. And if I did feel it, it wasn't the same way in which, or for the same reason, they felt it. If I had to break it down psychologically, I'd imagine that they felt, "Oh no, I actually got someone on the phone. This is my chance. I should nail it. I won't get someone on the phone for another 90 dials." Or, even more likely, they simply had a sales quota they needed to hit and felt some form of self-imposed pressure. Equally likely, they had a sales manager pushing them to their breaking point, micromanaging results out of them.

Most often, what they failed to realize was that I rarely—if ever—shared their sense of urgency. We were talking. *Correction: They were talking; I was listening.* But I wanted them to understand me. I wanted them to really understand me and what I was looking for help with. Yet to no avail, after a 30-minute call where they usually only highlighted a wide variety of facts and figures about their business and their customer base, they would eventually transition into asking me questions about my budget, who had decision-making power, and when we could "get a demo" or presentation booked. And I wasn't just talking to appointment-setters or sales development reps. Of course, at least when I was in the process of purchasing software, I was always talking to a "development" specialist and would be set up with an "expert" afterward. This is the salesforce model (as discussed in *Predictable Revenue*[4]); it's also a model many, many software businesses use today, including HubSpot. I like the notion that businesses are separating prospecting work from closing new business, but that is just one step in creating an efficient sales model, not an inbound sales model.

I acutely found all of this to be true when I was speaking with software sales reps. I hated it. From my experience, the worst part about this is *not* that I had to go through a "them-focused" sales process with the rep. Instead, they were creating a far more profound problem that would likely last beyond their tenure as a sales rep. Whether they realized it or not, they were literally shaping buyers' expectations of what it was like to buy from all salespeople. They were unintentionally manipulating buyers to believe that all reps only ask surface level questions. They were forming the perception that you could expect a sales rep to know his or her pitch, quote price, and ask for a sale, but rarely consult on real business issues contextualized to the buyer's unique challenges and organizational constraints. They were continuing, if not cementing, the damning legacy that all sales reps just want to get buyers on the phone, understand their budget, their decision-making power, and move to the sale as quickly as possible.

Inbound selling, in contrast, flips this paradigm on its head. Much the same way that inbound marketing can be defined as any form of marketing designed to earn a buyer's trust, inbound selling is any form of selling designed to earn a prospect's trust. It is the embodiment of salespeople changing the way they interact with prospects to match the way purchasing decisions are made in the twenty-first century. It is a mindset and a philosophy routed in empathy, well executed through person-alization and prioritizing a buyer's needs and goals over the seller's—always, and without exception.

One of my favorite analogies to make this form of selling more relatable is to take the Fight Club approach to sales: the first rule of inbound selling is that you do not talk about your company, product, or service until you absolutely must (for those of you who haven't seen the film *Fight Club*, or don't know what it is, the first rule of Fight Club is that you don't talk about Fight Club).

When you do eventually talk about your company, you keep it as concise as possible. There's a time and place for talking about your business and how you help, but the first one or two calls or meetings you have with a prospect are usually not the times to do it, at least not at length, unless the prospect asks those types of questions specifically. Instead, you must give or create something of value before you get anything back from your prospective customer. How?

The Inbound Sales Process and Inbound Sales Methodology

Almost half of all sales teams do not have a documented sales process. But, the sales teams that *do* follow a clear sales process are 33% more likely to be high performers, and their win rate exceeds 50% for two-thirds of companies that have a defined process in place.[5]

By now, I hope this is common knowledge. But if you're working on a team that does not have a sales process, or if you're leading a team that does not have a documented process, I'll share the one I know with you. Take heed, this is not going to be a drag and drop approach—nor should it be. I'm not advocating a cookie-cutter sales process. If every company used the exact same sales process, you would be giving up a major point of competitive differentiation. So instead, take some bits, pieces, nuts, or bolts from this one and then customize to your own business and to your own buyers.

Keep in mind, too, that while reading this many things you are about to read come directly from the team at HubSpot. They were the ones to create the inbound sales methodology and the inbound sales process;[6] I am simply the practitioner layering myself into the equation to provide deeper content, color, and context around how it all works. In no way does HubSpot necessarily endorse, nor does it follow the inbound sales

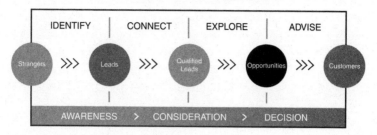

FIGURE 2.1 Inbound Sales Methodology
Source: Courtesy of HubSpot.

methodology the way I'll discuss it or lay it out in this book. Last, before I walk you through the entire inbound sales methodology and associated process, I'll highlight how it all works at a high level.

The inbound sales methodology is a four-part framework that transforms selling to match the way people buy today. It comprises four specific types of actions that salespeople must take as their prospective buyers move throughout their journey—from Awareness to Consideration, and ultimately Decision. Done successfully, this series of actions—above all else—supports the prospect through the Buyer's Journey, and ultimately, in moving qualified leads into opportunities and eventually customers.

The Inbound Sales Methodology[7]

In the following chapters, I'll dig into each of the four core actions associated with the inbound sales methodology (see Figure 2.1).

Part 2

How to Be an Inbound Seller: A Playbook for the Front-Line Sales Rep

Chapter 3

Identify

How to Identify the Right People and Businesses to Pursue

To change the way you sell to match how people buy, you are better off starting your sales activities by engaging active buyers. These are individuals who have already entered the Awareness stage of the buyer's journey. This means speaking with individuals who have already *self*-identified that they may have a problem they're trying to solve, as opposed to you solely identifying that they look and feel like the type of company you want to, or should, sell to.

An inbound seller can pick up on clues that the buyer has entered the Awareness stage of the buyer's journey by looking for signs that someone has visited your company's website, filled out a form on the site (e.g., registered for a webinar, downloaded an e-book, etc.), opened a recent email from the company, engaged with certain pieces of content on LinkedIn, and more. By taking this approach, you are more likely to seam yourself into a conversation with a person who is in a receptive, learning mindset as opposed to interrupting someone who has their attention focused on anything other than speaking with you.

Moreover, inbound sellers should primarily talk to good-fit customers, inbound leads, and inbound companies. Yet, I can tell you that, as a practitioner, this approach will lead to failure for an inbound seller unless the business has already defined what "good fit" means, is generating inbound leads or inbound companies, and has crafted the messaging to reach out to said "fits," leads, and companies. So that's exactly where we'll start—understanding how to define buyer fit before practicing inbound sales.

How to Define Buyer Fit Before Practicing Inbound Sales

Somewhat surprisingly, disagreement about the ideal buyer is one of the most common disconnects between sales and marketing teams. This notion is further supported by research from the Corporate Executive Board, which states the number one reason that companies lack alignment in sales and marketing is because the sales and marketing teams do not have a shared vision or understanding of their customer.[1]

Even if your company intends to continue selling to many types of businesses, it's critical to focus on one buyer type at a time when doing things like crafting messaging, creating content, building campaigns, and designing sales processes. Otherwise, you look like you're trying to be "everything to everyone," and as a result, your sales and marketing won't resonate with anyone.

At HubSpot, the two primary tools we use to cut through this fog—and teach all our customers to use—are called *buyer profiles* and *buyer personas*. In short, think of a buyer's profile as a definition of the type of company to target, while a buyer's persona is the individual within that company. They are stereotypes—in the best sense of the word—of what your ideal buyer or customer "looks" like.

For those of you in the B2C world, you wouldn't be doing the buyer profile and instead would skip ahead to articulating your buyer persona or buyer personas (assuming you have more than one type of ideal buyer and they are distinctly different from one another). Next is my recommendation on how to build out each at your own business.

How to Build a Buyer Profile

When starting to define your buyer profile, get a group of people together from your sales and marketing teams at a minimum. Of course, you may want to invite more team members from services, support, engineering, and account management as well, but at least start with sales and marketing.

Once you get the team together, remember that the criteria used to describe the ideal buyer profile will be different at different companies, but most businesses will have some common criteria, such as size of company, industry, and geographic location.

For each of these criteria, think through what the ideal is. For company size, is a big company better served than a small company? Is a company that is based in a specific region of the world a better fit for your products or services than a company in another region?

Start this group exercise by asking an open-ended question, *"Which criteria define an ideal target customer for you?"* Once you've facilitated a bit of a conversation, ask stakeholders to write their ideas down on a simple worksheet divided into two columns. Ask them to write their criteria in the first column and the characteristics in the second. Figure 3.1 shows what the output of that exercise might look like.

The output of this process should be a simple description of the ideal company your business sells to and serves—a definition that starts to align both the sales and marketing teams. Using the Example Buyer Profile Exercise Worksheet, here's an example definition: *A software or IT hardware company that has between 25 and 200 employees that sells direct to other businesses and uses Gmail as their business email provider.*

Naturally, you'll probably have trouble getting all your company's stakeholders to agree on a narrower target. If the

Criteria	Characteristic	Importance (pick 5)
Company size	25–200 employees	2
Company size	200–2,000 employees	
Sells to	Other businesses	1
Industry	Software	4
Industry	IT hardware	5
Go-to-Market	Sells direct	
Uses software	Gmail	3

FIGURE **3.1**   Example Buyer Profile Exercise Worksheet
Source: Courtesy of HubSpot.

"ideal buyer profile" is too broad, and you can't get group agreement, create multiple profiles. Once you've defined these multiple profiles, prioritize and focus on who to target first, second, third, and so on. Ultimately, you'll want to use these profiles to build out marketing content and either design or modify your company's sales process.

HOW TO BUILD A BUYER PERSONA
Now that we've laid out some simple tools to build the buyer profile, it's time to define the ideal buyer persona. Remember, at the end of the day, people buy things, and to earn their attention and interest, we must make our sales and marketing messages highly relevant to them at the right time. To make them relevant, we build buyer personas before implementing the inbound sales methodology.

To do this, you'll follow virtually the same process you went through to build a buyer profile. However, there is going to be one key difference. Instead of just documenting demographic information that describes the company, like industry, number of employees, or geographic region, you need to start getting into the head of your prospective buyer. You can keep this very high level or make it very specific. If you haven't done this before, I'd encourage you to keep it high level. But whatever you do, it must be personal and specific to an individual within the ideal buyer profile company.

As a clarifying point, when I say, "Get in their heads," I specifically mean that I want you and your team to think about things such as:

- What are this person's goals at work?
- How are they measured for their performance?
- In relation to work, what keeps them up at night?
- If you could visualize this person's to-do list, what would the top three things on it likely be?
- How does *your* company help them solve their problems and achieve their goals?

You might even get more detailed and begin to explore personal questions such as:

- What's their personal life like?
- Do they work long hours or short ones?
- Do they work remotely or in an office?
- What are the nuances that might make their job particularly difficult in their industry or function?

Your level of understanding on these points will enable deep customization of marketing campaigns and the sales process, which drives better outcomes for buyers and sellers alike (not to mention you'll make your marketing team *very* happy). The more specific you can be when building buyer personas, the more it will help your marketing team attract inbound leads and companies, which as an inbound seller you will come to cherish every single day. Equally important, this level of specificity is going to empower you to tailor your communication with prospects, which, when done well, instills trust, confidence, and differentiation in the eyes of your buyer. It is at the heart of inbound selling.

Just like ideal buyer profiles, most companies eventually target more than one person. If there is more than one buyer persona heavily involved in a buying decision within the target company—and there likely will be considering the average B2B purchasing process incudes over six (6!) people now— you should create two or more personas.[2] For example, one persona might be focused on a "VP of Sales," while another might be a "Sales Manager."

In other words, don't expect to define your persona perfectly on your first sitting, and remember to focus on one buyer persona at a time early on. The more buyer personas you create, the more you must distribute time and resources to build marketing campaigns and tailor the sales process associated with each persona.

One last thought I'll share on building buyer personas and buyer profiles: Another method for setting buyer profiles and personas is to examine the characteristics of existing customers or contacts in your existing sales and marketing database. These contacts can be analyzed through simple methods, such as:

- One-on-one interviews with existing customers (highly recommended)
- A survey
- Analysis of data that your company has about its customers (for example, in your CRM. If you don't have a CRM, HubSpot gives one away for free and you can get it here: https://www.hubspot.com/products/crm)
- Capturing information about leads or customers when they come back to download content or engage with your website (if you don't have a way to do this now, HubSpot also gives away free tools to track this activity: https://www.hubspot.com/products/marketing)

Now that you've done the hard work of building out the buyer profiles and personas, it's important not to skip some final critical steps.

DOCUMENT WHAT YOU'VE DEVELOPED FOR BOTH THE BUYER PROFILE AND BUYER PERSONA

Ensure that the profiles and personas are clearly documented, shared, and socialized within your organization. Again, at a minimum, this information needs to be shared within the sales and marketing organizations but should ideally get socialized within every business function. The "second tier" of functions will likely include account management, support, customer service, and more, depending on your business. Moreover, I would argue that you should include these individuals in the buyer profile and buyer persona development process to the extent possible; individuals working in these roles have just as much valuable insight into your customers and are by no means second-class corporate citizens.

Everyone that works at your company should have an intimate understanding of *who* you are helping and *how* you help them. Figure 3.2 shows an example of a template from HubSpot[3] to document and share demographic information.

SHARE WHAT YOU'VE LEARNED ABOUT YOUR PERSONA'S MOTIVATIONS

This is where you'll distill the information you learned from asking why so much during your group discussions or interviews, if you built personas using that method. What keeps your persona up at night? Who do they want to be? Most important, tie that all together by telling people how your company can help them (see Figure 3.3).

ENSURE THE SALES TEAM IS PREPARED FOR CONVERSATIONS WITH YOUR PERSONA

Include some real quotes from your persona-building exercises or interviews that exemplify what your personas are concerned

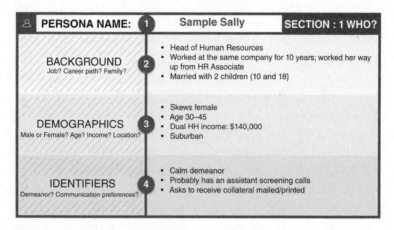

FIGURE 3.2   HubSpot Buyer Persona Example: Who?
Source: Courtesy of HubSpot.

about, who they are, and what they want. Then create a list of the questions, goals, challenges, objections or concerns they might raise so your sales team is prepared to address those during their conversations with prospects (see Figure 3.4). This

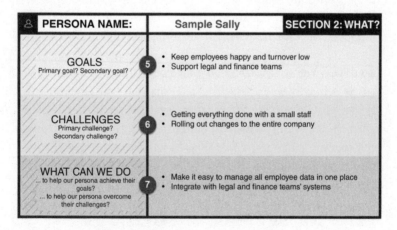

FIGURE 3.3   HubSpot Buyer Persona Example: What?
Source: Courtesy of HubSpot.

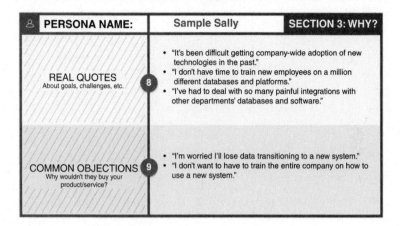

 👤 **PERSONA NAME:**	**Sample Sally**	**SECTION 3: WHY?**
REAL QUOTES About goals, challenges, etc. ⑧	• "It's been difficult getting company-wide adoption of new technologies in the past." • "I don't have time to train new employees on a million different databases and platforms." • "I've had to deal with so many painful integrations with other departments' databases and software."	
COMMON OBJECTIONS ⑨ Why wouldn't they buy your product/service?	• "I'm worried I'll lose data transitioning to a new system." • "I don't want to have to train the entire company on how to use a new system."	

FIGURE 3.4 HubSpot Buyer Persona Example: Why?

Source: Courtesy of HubSpot.

is a critical step, that if missed, will lead the sales team to fail. They need to be able to add value to the potential customer's life before attempting to extract it; this is the expectation of the modern, empowered buyer.

HELP CRAFT MESSAGING FOR YOUR PERSONA

Tell people how to talk about your products/services with your persona. This includes the detailed vernacular you should use, as well as a more general elevator pitch that positions your solution in a way that resonates with your persona. For example, when I was selling into marketing agencies, I rarely ever used the word "sales"; instead, I referred to sales as "business development." This is a tiny tweak in vocabulary that only comes through understanding your prospective customers but will make all the difference in your ability to build trust with them. Taking this step also ensures everyone in your company is speaking the same language when they're having conversations with leads and customers (see Figure 3.5). Early on in a company's development, this may not be at the top of the

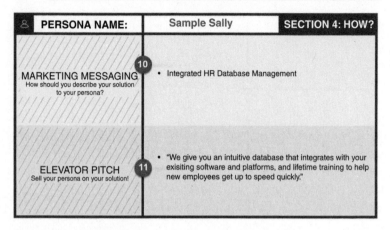

FIGURE 3.5 HubSpot Buyer Persona Example: How?

Source: Courtesy of HubSpot.

priority list. But as a company scales to hundreds, or thousands, of employees, it's non-negotiable.

NAME YOUR PERSONAS

Finally, make sure you give your persona a name (like Finance Manager Margie, IT Ian, or Landscaper Larry) and include a real-life image of your persona so everyone can truly envision what he or she looks like. Ideally, don't use a photo stock image—use a picture from a real customer (with their permission, ideally) to bring her to life. I realize this may sound juvenile, but the true value in naming the persona is that it serves as a quick mental trigger to recall information for anyone inside your business, and establishes common language across the organization.

If you've gone this far, you already have a good grasp of the Identify phase. However, it doesn't stop there. You still need to think about whom specifically you are going to call. If you're fortunate enough to have a killer marketing team generating inbound leads and companies for you, and ideally passing you lead intelligence about how they've interacted with your marketing, then you'll have a big head start. If you don't, don't worry. Yet.

We've Documented, Shared, and Socialized Everything. What's Next?

It's time to start implementing the inbound sales methodology, but not without doing a little more research and preparation as an inbound seller. You're probably looking for a starting point on who to call and how to approach them, so here are some of the steps I went through as a rep, assuming you already have leads that have been generated by your marketing team. If you don't, keep reading, and I'll cover how to leverage inbound companies.

On the account or company record that you want to initiate a discussion with:

Are There Single or Many Contacts Already in the Database? I would look to see whether there have been multiple contacts from the prospect's company that engaged with my company or just one. As is outlined in Ross's *Predictable Revenue*, we know that the person we need to start the conversation with is often difficult to identify, and the person we typically need to speak with to make a purchasing decision is not the person we are going to start our sales discovery process with.

How Recent and How Frequent Are Their Interactions with Your Company? When was the last time this person (or people) was on my company's website? What did they look at? Was it a top of the funnel piece of content (blog post, e-book, webinar, or something else)? Or was it a bottom of the funnel piece of content (free consultation request, demo request, pricing page view, started a free trial, or something else)? Knowing this makes a difference because it is going to give me a sense of where they are in the buyer's journey

(Awareness –> Consideration –> Decision). It will also help me understand how much self-education they've done versus how much I may need to do with them. No amount is "bad," I just don't want to overconsult or underconsult. I should find the Goldilocks amount of information to prepare and context to provide, and that's no easy task.

Am I Targeting a Core Buyer Persona or Are There Micro Buyer Personas? Your business may have a buyer persona or buyer personas developed, but there are probably multiple subsets of buyers. For example, at HubSpot we have a few core buyer personas. Marketing Mary, a marketing manager at a midsized organization; Corporate Cathy, a marketing manager or CMO at a slightly larger organization; Agency Erin, a marketing agency owner looking to grow and scale her business; and the list goes on.

But within "Agency Erin," for example, we have five subpersonas. Those personas revolve around the slightly nuanced business challenges that different types of marketing services agencies might face. For example, a website development firm is likely to struggle with cash-flow issues, while an SEO/PPC/social agency is probably struggling to grow the size of their retainers and prove ROI to customers. And because their challenges differ, I'm going to position my conversation differently. I need to tailor that conversation and add value by demonstrating my knowledge of their business to earn their trust.

What Are the General Business Demographics? Last, of course, I want to understand some basic information about the types of businesses or people my prospect sells to, whether or not they are B2B or B2C, average sales price of their products/services, how many employees work at the business, how long the business has been around for (especially for small business), whether the company—or person—was mentioned in the news positively or negatively or won any awards, and I want to soak in as much information through their LinkedIn profile as possible. I will even look through the company's blog if they have one, or the company's or prospect's Twitter handle to see what they care about, who they interact with, and what types of information they're sharing.

What's this person's digital footprint? Even taking a few minutes to do a quick Google search, a look through the company website, and a review of their LinkedIn profile could reveal a great deal. Through Google, you may learn about recent company news. Through the website, you may see that this person has published content, which would be an easy way to start conversation and determine what they may care about. Or, LinkedIn will show you similar types of information around what the person cares about simply by reviewing their activity feed, or lack thereof. Equally important, it will show you whether you and this person share any mutual connections, and more.

Wait . . . Isn't This Going to Take F-O-R-E-V-E-R?

This entire research process—once you get your method down—should not take more than 5 or 10 minutes. Of course, if you're working large enterprise deals, you're going to want to spend even more time mapping out the account and opportunities that exist within it. Delegate as much as you can to your BDR/SDR, but coach them along the way on what types of information they should be looking for, especially if you're working in a named accounts model (for example, account-based marketing/selling).

Alternatively, if you're working a much larger territory or prospect universe, you're going to need to keep your activity levels high, so five to ten minutes should suffice. Early on, this could take you anywhere from ten to twenty minutes per prospective company. That's okay! As you progress, the time required for researching and synthesizing information will diminish. Moreover, attempting to communicate with 10 highly researched prospects is much better than working a hundred who you know nothing about.

What about Cold, or (Barely) Lukewarm Leads?

If you're wondering how to approach a cold lead, inbound company (a company that has visited your site but no leads have converted), or connect with someone on LinkedIn or Twitter, the answer is that it's mostly the same. The key difference is in how you open the conversation.

As opposed to leading with how that person was interacting with your company recently, you'll likely need to explain why you researched them and decided to call that person specifically and, of course, how you typically help people like them. Trigger events are especially helpful here, too. These are events such as a prospect being mentioned in the news, winning an award, a recent press release, a job change, a funding round (if you sell to startups, for example), acquiring another company, and so forth.

Mastering Follow Through as an Inbound Seller

I have heard a wide range of opinions on the right number of times, the right time, and the right days to connect with prospects. I'll share what I've learned here but will also sum it up with a few recommendations on effective prospecting.

♦ Beware of pure cold-calling; it's extremely rare to get someone you've never engaged with, or who has not engaged with you, to pick up an unknown call. In no way am I advocating that you do not ever pick up the phone, quite the opposite in fact. It's just that when you do, you should start with inbound leads (people who have expressed some level of interest in your company's content or your content), then move on to inbound companies (people who have visited your company's site but who have not filled out forms), and then move to everyone else. Ideally, you should be prioritizing in an order that looks something like Figure 3.6.

INTEREST

(As expressed through website or social engagement)

	SECOND	FIRST
PROSPECT FIT *(Relative to Your Buyer Profile/ Persona)*	FOURTH	THIRD

FIGURE 3.6 Prospect Prioritization Matrix

- Spend extra time crafting thoughtful, tailored emails *and* engaging prospects on social media—note that I emphasized the "and"; do not just email or try to connect with prospects on social—do both.
- Listen, engage, and add value first; ask for the meeting later. In fact, some of the most effective prospecting messages I've received via email or LinkedIn specifically call out that there is no ask whatsoever in the message. Don't do this, just appreciate the concept.
- Be intelligently persistent; the average rep gives up after one or two attempts, but 80% of all sales are initiated after five or more attempts to connect with a prospect.[4]

Data from InsightSquared suggest that while the first three to four rounds of attempts have the highest likelihood of connecting, the connect rate still stays right around 5% for attempt 6 all the way through attempt 11 and higher. In other words, the connect rate never drops to zero (see Figure 3.7).[5]

That said, before you jump out of your seat and start dialing, you need to have a plan. There are two core concepts behind this plan: (1) organization and (2) execution.

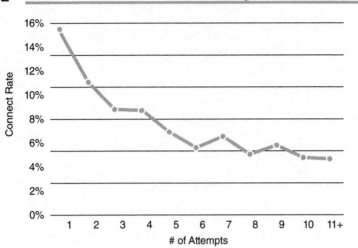

FIGURE 3.7   Connect Rate by Attempt
Source: Courtesy of InsightSquared.

Final Planning Steps before You Attempt to Engage Anyone, in Any Way

BASIC ORGANIZATIONAL CHECKLIST

Organization means that you are literally prepared to start prospecting. Ask yourself these questions:

- ◆ Do you have your lead views or contact views set up?
- ◆ Do you have your email templates ready and have a sense of how to customize templates?
- ◆ Do you know exactly how you want to deliver a voicemail?
- ◆ Are you truly calling at the right time?
- ◆ Do you know exactly what you want to achieve on the connect call if a prospect picks up or returns your call?
- ◆ What's your plan to engage the prospect beyond phone and email? If I told you phone and email wasn't an option—which is completely possible in the future—

what would you do? Hint: Think website chat and think social (LinkedIn).

If you don't have answers to these questions, get them. And if you don't have them, I'll share some thoughts on how I went about doing this myself and how the best inside sales reps I've worked with go about this.

CREATING VIEWS OF LEADS AND CONTACTS

As far as creating lead views goes, I recommend rating your leads before you call them. Prioritize by "SQL/MQL/PQL" versus "White Bread Lead" first. For the sake of simplicity, an "SQL/MQL/PQL" means any lead who has shown a high level of interest with your company in some way (think: "contact sales form completed" or "website chat initiated" or has visited your company's product or pricing page) and who fits the buyer persona well. A "White Bread Lead" is typically someone who may fit the buyer persona well, but hasn't demonstrated much interest with your business from an activity perspective (i.e., website visits, page views, content downloads, social interactions, etc.).

Second, prioritize by amount of downtime since last interaction, if any. If your company offers you any lead scoring, you might want to take that into account as well, but remember that a lead scoring model is only as good as the person that built it. If you don't feel confident that your marketing team has built the lead score the right way, talk with them about it. Figure out what goes into that score, and if you have a different view, share it. Believe me—they should want to help you find the "most likely to close" leads.

ACTUAL OUTREACH—ATTEMPTING CONTACT!

Execution—the second component—which includes when to call and what to say, is both easy and difficult. I'll also provide some guidance on how to structure what you're going to say (*not the literal script for what* you're going to say—this should be on your SVP, VP, director, manager, you, or all of the above).

At HubSpot, we followed the Basho methodology.[6] Defined by HubSpot, this is a progression of messages (voicemails and emails, though today it includes more such as website chat, direct meetings booked, and social interactions) that is meant to gain a prospect's attention through repetition and continuous accretion of value. Until the breakup message.

A strong Basho sequence is:

- Composed of at least six steps
- Executed every other, or every third business day—designed to last a total of 10 to 15 business days
- Followed up immediately with an email that is virtually identical to the voicemail left for the contact or lead
- Leverages the word "you" often
- Concludes with a "break up" of the communication stream

Here's the exact Basho sequence I used at HubSpot for two years as a rep. Keep in mind that the email and voicemail scripts are almost identical to reinforce the message or increase the chance that the message is understood. If your company allows you to replace the phone with channels such as LinkedIn and Twitter, this will increase your chances of getting a response. If they don't allow you to eliminate the phone altogether, but still allow social media interaction, then layer in social as a third prospecting activity type. And of course, if your company leverages website chat, make sure you're all over that.

Again, *do not just copy and paste* this content. Use the nature and structure of messages like these, but tailor them to your own business, your own sales process, and to the unique buyer profiles and buyer personas your company serves.

Basho #1

Subject Line: Did you find everything you were looking for help with?

Hi [CONTACT FIRST NAME],

You recently visited our website and expressed interest in some of HubSpot's content.

Since we haven't had a chance to connect live, is there a good time for you to speak?

I wanted to spend about 10 minutes on the phone learning more about you and your firm to determine whether you might be a good fit for our partner program for marketing agencies.

What does your schedule look like?

Best,

Basho #2

Subject Line: HubSpot Partner Program | {!Lead. Company}

Hi [CONTACT FIRST NAME],

You recently requested some information on HubSpot and I wanted to follow up and see if you found everything you were looking for help with.

I work with marketing agencies, web design firms, and PR consultants through HubSpot's Agency Partner Team,

---

and based on your website it looks like you could potentially be a good fit for our Partner Program: www.hubspot.com/agency-partners.

Please let me know if you have 10–15 minutes to chat this week, and we can both determine whether it makes sense to explore a partnership.

Best,

Basho #3

Subject Line: How HubSpot Helps Agencies Grow

Hi [CONTACT FIRST NAME],

You recently expressed an interest in HubSpot and some of our content.

I thought I'd reach out because through our partner program for firms like yours, we've helped many of our partners expand and grow their businesses in a variety of ways. Here's the link to our partner homepage: www .hubspot.com/partners.

Our Partner Program has helped marketing agencies with the following areas:

1. *Measuring Client ROI—Predicting, measuring, and delivering a stronger ROI from the online marketing services you provide*
2. *Internal Lead Generation—Signing up more clients faster by generating more leads for your services and improving your sales processes*

3. *Services Expansion—Developing or improving your online marketing services offering*
4. *Shifting to Retainer-Based Engagements—Generating a larger portion of your revenue from bigger recurring retainers*
5. *Agency Sales Training—Becoming an expert at SEO, social media, closed loop marketing analytics, business blogging, lead generation, and marketing automation*

Are you looking for help with any of the above?

If so, let me know if you'd like to chat over the phone to learn more. My number is [FILL IN YOUR PHONE NUMBER].

Best,

Basho #4

Subject Line: Educational Materials from HubSpot for Marketing Companies

Hi [CONTACT FIRST NAME],

After you downloaded some of our free educational materials, I sent you several emails. I've reached out because it seems like we'd be able to help your business like we've helped other marketing agencies.

I also shared with you several areas in the HubSpot Partner Program that marketing agencies leverage to grow their business. Are you looking for help with any of the areas I shared with you?

> *I also pointed you to some additional free training resources we've produced specifically to help marketing agencies grow their sales, expand their services offerings and improve the ROI they deliver to their clients:* http:// offers.hubspot.com/5-core-services-of-inbound-marketing.
>
> *If you review those resources and have questions or feel we can help you, I'd invite you to start a free trial (* http:// offers.hubspot.com/free-trial-ad) *and begin exploring.*
>
> *Or, feel free to just reach out to me.*
>
> *Regards,*

Basho #5

> *Subject Line: Should I Stay or Should I Go?*
>
> *Hi [CONTACT FIRST NAME], per my message today –*
>
> *I've tried to reach you a few times but haven't heard back from you and that tells me one of three things:*
>
> 1. *You're all set and have no interest in the HubSpot Partner Program to grow your business, and if that's the case please let me know so can I stop bothering you.*
> 2. *You're still interested but haven't had the time to get back to me yet.*
> 3. *You've fallen and can't get up, in which case please let me know and I'll call 911 for you.*

> *Please let me know which one it is because I'm starting to worry.*
>
> *Thanks in advance and I look forward to hearing back from you!*
>
> *Regards,*

Basho #6

> *Subject Line: If You Change Your Mind about Becoming a HubSpot Partner*
>
> *Hi [CONTACT FIRST NAME],*
>
> *I've reached out several times to you and have not heard back. You seemed like a good candidate for our partner program for marketing agencies:* http://www.hubspot.com/partners
>
> *I don't believe I've received a response from you. And I don't think you've started a free trial of our software (*http://offers.hubspot.com/free-trial-ad*).*
>
> *So, at this point, I'll assume that you don't need our help with anything.*
>
> *My contact information is below if anything changes for you.*
>
> *Regards,*

When Should I Try to Connect with My Prospect?

The Lead Response Management Organization did a beautiful research study on this topic, which was very well summarized by the team at InsightSquared on this very topic.[7] This is the full blog post if you want to read it directly: http://www.insightsquared .com/2014/02/what-is-the-best-time-for-cold-calls/.

In short, here's my call to action for all sales reps—throw conventional wisdom out the door! If you want a break, come in late or leave early, depending on what time zone you're calling into of course. Here's why:

First, what's interesting is that InsightSquared, using their own data as a sample set, found that what they held as conventional wisdom—that prospects are more likely to engage with you early in the day—is not true. Instead, they saw their best connect rate between the hours of 10:00 a.m. and 4:00 p.m. (see Figure 3.8).

Second, they dug deeper into which day of the week is the most effective to drive the highest volume of connects. Short

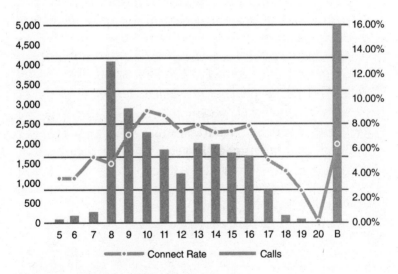

Figure 3.8 Best Time of Day for Sales Calls

Source: Courtesy of InsightSquared.

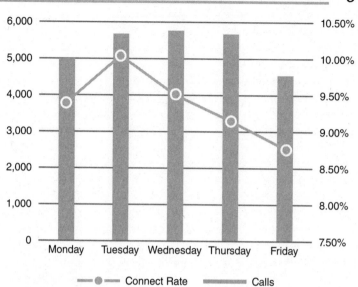

FIGURE 3.9 Best Day of the Week for Sales Calls
Source: Courtesy of InsightSquared.

answer? Tuesday (see Figure 3.9). Of course, I'm not recommending you *only* prospect on Tuesday; instead, I'm just saying you should make sure you don't put prospecting on the backburner on Tuesdays.

For me, I would personally worry much less about the exact time and day that you call, and worry much more about the channels you use (ideally, website chat, email, social, and phone [for inbound leads]) and what you say when you attempt to reach out. Don't get lost in the time of day or day of the week; there are just too many variables that could disprove these generalizations when attempted on a prospect-by-prospect basis.

Now that you've learned how to identify the right people to contact and how to attempt connecting with them, let's dive into the true beginning of the inbound sales process—the connect call. This is the first time you speak meaningfully with your prospective buyer.

Chapter 4

Connect

How to Engage Active—and Not So Active—Buyers

At the end of my second week in training at HubSpot, we started to have a good deal of free time. I remember asking my manager, Dannie, what I should be doing. She recommended I read a lot of our customer case studies, listen to recorded calls from other sales reps, read the sales playbook, and watch training videos on our sales process.

I completed that work in an afternoon, taking copious notes the way a good researcher would. The next day I explained to her that I had completed the task at hand and, in the back of my mind, expected praise for it. Instead, I got the opposite. Maybe not the opposite of praise, but perhaps some tough love.

I proudly walked over to Dannie's desk, announced that I had finished my homework assignment, and asked, "So what else can I be doing?" Her response was perfect, but scared the hell out of me: "Sig, I recommend you get on the phone and start calling people who expressed interest in HubSpot, or our content. That's what we hired you to do, isn't it?"

Now take what I'm about to tell you with a grain of salt. I went back to my desk, sat down, opened our CRM, and pulled up my lead view, titled "My New Leads."

At HubSpot, we're spoiled. Especially in 2012, we were *very* spoiled. I asked for leads and the marketing gods just provided.

There were literally tens of thousands of leads for us to call because our marketing team relentlessly created high-quality content to attract visitors to our site and convert them into leads. That was the part of the business development process I understood. It was everything that came *after* that that was a true mystery to me. However, that mystery was about to be solved.

With my headset on, glass of water full, desk clear, notepad out, pen ready, glasses on, lead record up, and the lead's LinkedIn profile up, I was ready. Then it all hit me like a ton of bricks . . . I panicked.

What was I doing here? Why did I agree to be in sales? I *hated* doing research calls with customers when I was an analyst at CEB. I needed coaching all the time back then to nail my calls. I didn't even want to call leads when I was at GiftsOnTime. I hated calling the vendors and "pitching" them on what we had to bring to the table. I got sweaty palms before all of our trade shows. "I shouldn't be here!" I screamed to myself. It got worse. I realized that not only had my confidence vanished, the sales floor was deafeningly loud. It was all-out hysteria.

On top of that, the guy across from me, who also became a very good friend, had a standing desk, and it was as if he was yelling right at me while I was trying to make calls. I couldn't do this. I was supposed to be researching things. Writing things. Listening to classic rock while I cranked out executive insights, research briefs, and case studies. "I was not supposed to be here!" my inner voice screamed. Yet somehow, I managed to hit the headset button on my phone and I heard a dial tone. It was go time.

To this day, I still don't know how I managed to make that first call, but I did. Not only that, the person picked up! I was pissed! I thought for sure I would get a chance to leave a few voicemails, send a few emails, and "loosen up" before I had to have an "actual" conversation with a "real" person! But no, David had to answer. We talked for about 10 minutes and I managed to book another call with him.

I got off the phone and couldn't believe I managed to get through it. It felt painful. I wasn't ready for it. I had no idea what I was doing. I pulled up the activity leaderboard and I stood at one—count it—one sales attempt for the day. Most reps at the time were cranking out over a hundred attempts daily; the best well into the 120s and 130s.

I picked up the phone and made another call. And again, another person picked up on the other end! I couldn't believe this! People aren't supposed to pick up phone calls from sales reps! What were they thinking? That conversation didn't go as well, so I sent some follow-ups and never heard from that person again, and I assure you it wasn't for lack of persistence.

The third time around I thought, "Surely, there's no way this person is going to pick up the phone. You're going to get a chance to leave a bunch of emails and voicemails, you'll get into a groove, you'll get your activity up, and you'll connect with some people tomorrow. Tomorrow will be better. It will all be fine."

Of course, I was wrong again. The third lead picked up the phone, and there I was—living a true trial by fire—no idea what I was supposed to be doing. This went on for a couple more weeks, but in that time, I realized a few important things:

- ♦ Once you start calling, it gets exponentially easier. It becomes like breathing.
- ♦ After you make enough attempts, you start to learn what it is you're doing wrong and you can course correct.
- ♦ In that barrage of activity, you start to sound polished. You sound like you know what you're talking about. And the reality is that you probably do know what you're talking about even if you don't feel that way.

My advice for anyone with a fear of dialing, or trying to get into a rhythm of attempts, is to keep this guidance in mind:

- Your prospects are just people.
- You had a good reason (or should) to call or contact them in the first place.
- You will get better over time.
- You need to "flip a lot of stones" to "find your diamonds"—even if someone is strongly aligned with your company's buyer profile or persona(s), it doesn't mean they're a good fit to work with you right now.
- You should act like you know what you're doing, even if you don't, and your knowledge will catch up with your "acting" quickly.

The way these conversations started, however, was what really struck me as different relative to what I had experienced on the other side of the phone in the past. Stripping away all else, I was calling them because they started the conversation. They were the ones that came to our website. They were the ones that filled out our landing page form for an e-book, guide, checklist, and so on. They were the ones that filled out the form with real contact information. So, my "pitch" wasn't really a pitch at all. My opening line every time I called someone was (and still is),

> *"Hi [PROSPECT], You came to HubSpot's website and downloaded [XYZ CONTENT]. Is there something you were looking for help with?"*

This opening line was game changing back then. Why? Because it does not require you to pitch anything, whatsoever. Whoever you're calling came to your website and was looking for help with something regardless of whether they're willing to admit it. That said, your call will still probably go something like this:

PROSPECT: "Hello? Who is this?"

YOU: "Hi [PROSPECT], I saw that you came to our website and downloaded [CONTENT] on [TOPIC]. Is there something you were looking for help with?"

PROSPECT: "Where are you calling from?"

YOU: "[COMPANY NAME]. My marketing team sent me a message because you were on our website somewhat recently and downloaded [CONTENT]. I thought I would follow up to see what you were researching and if I could point you in the right direction."

PROSPECT: "Oh, yeah, now I remember. I did download [CONTENT] but I haven't had time to read through it. It's sitting on my desk in a stack of papers now. Can you call me back some other time or send me an email?"

YOU: "Understood. I could call you back, but I have a couple of minutes now and could save you the hassle of reading the [CONTENT]."

The conversation may go on and on like this for a bit. Key to being successful is making sure you position yourself as a "helper" first, above all else. I can't reinforce this enough—inbound selling is helpful, not hostile.

If you lay on a pitch, start talking about your company, start asking probing questions that the prospect isn't ready to answer—and frankly, questions that you have not yet earned the right to ask—you will miss sales opportunity after sales opportunity. You need to find ways to *give* before you *get*.

Why do I believe in this so much? I practiced the approach for years with success, and coached others to do the same, but it's also rooted in deep research done by one of the best management research companies in existence today—the Corporate Executive Board (acquired by Gartner in 2017).

WAIT . . . WHAT IF I DON'T HAVE ANY INBOUND LEADS!?

I realize some of you reading this don't have the luxury of inbound leads. I also understand that not all businesses have adopted the inbound marketing model; or, if they have, their lead flow isn't heavy enough to warrant 100% of the sales organization focusing on inbound selling. However, I would be willing to bet that most businesses have at least some sort of a marketing list that they can use to start driving inbound leads.

Furthermore, my advice to any sales rep that is not currently benefitting from inbound leads: After building your business case, go to your sales director and VP, and discuss the benefits and drawback of your company adopting an inbound marketing approach, even if only partially. If you want help with explaining why, I would start here: How to Prove the Value of Inbound to Your CFO [Free Kit]: http://blog.hubspot.com/marketing/inbound-marketing-cfo-prove-value[1]. If that approach is just too big a mountain to climb, here are some alternative ways you can become an inbound seller, faster.

REFLECT ON THE QUESTIONS YOUR BUYERS HAVE ALREADY ASKED YOU

Sit down for an hour and ask yourself, "What are the most common questions that prospects ask?" If you have not been on enough sales calls to know, listen to other reps' calls. Or, just ask other reps what types of questions prospects are asking. Take it a step further and start asking yourself exactly which challenges your company solves for. Think about how your prospect might articulate that challenge in the form of a question.

Your Very Own Email Inbox Is a Goldmine

One of the easiest places to go—not only for the questions, but for the answers too—is your own email inbox. Think about how many times you've answered questions for prospects who weren't quite ready, willing, or able to get on a phone call with you. I bet it's more than a handful. Find those email exchanges, at a bare minimum, to seed the list of questions you should be building.

Flipping Questions into Statements = Baseline Content

Once you've created that list of challenges or questions (I would recommend starting with +/− 20 challenges/questions)—simply turn those questions into statements. For example, **challenge**: "How do I generate more leads on Twitter?" Turned into a **statement**: "How to generate more leads on Twitter."

You can even take this further, putting some sales and marketing "flare" on it: "**The three most effective ways** to generate leads on Twitter." Again, remember that even though you are writing this as a statement, it originated as a question. Better yet, coming back to your email as a source, you may already have the answers to those questions right under your nose!

Sharing Your Perspective on Those Challenges Is a Requirement, *Not* an Option

Now that you've turned your questions into statements, it's time to either start or join the conversation about those challenges. Easy ways to do this include:

1. **Create your own personal blog, use Medium, or ask to be published on your company's blog and publish 1 to 2 posts per month**. The article doesn't have to be perfect. Just write it and ship it. You should write no more than 800 to 1,200 words on this and it

should not take you more than 1 to 2 hours to write. If you don't want to write, have someone interview you (or "interview" yourself), record it, and send it to a transcription service like Rev.

2. **Don't want to manage a blog?** At a bare minimum, publish your articles to your LinkedIn profile using long-format content. An amazing saleswoman I've worked with for years, Ali, does this incredibly well, even though she would be more than capable maintaining her own blog to boot. This is a highly effective way to give yourself even more exposure to prospective buyers than you would have otherwise.

3. **Are you too busy to write?** The sales reps that are going to win in the twenty-first century are those that are the most knowledgeable and most helpful. You need to start helping your prospects answer their questions right now. But, if you truly have writer's block (which I'm convinced per a speech from Seth Godin does not exist because there's no such thing as "talker's block"), join LinkedIn groups and start following the blogs that your prospects are a part of and follow. Make sure you join the conversation and add value. Offer a new perspective. Share industry insights and stats. Do storytelling. And remember, *do not* promote your company. Inbound selling is predicated on leading with value. Again, you must give, and give feverishly, before you will be able or deserving of a "get."

4. **Promote your knowledge and ability to help others more broadly**. Again, do not promote your business specifically. I cannot stress this enough. But if you do write a new article, have an insight on a new piece of news that came out in your industry, or a perspective on an article someone else has already

written, share it through social media. At a bare minimum, you need to be sharing through Twitter and LinkedIn. Even if you're convinced that your key decision-makers and stakeholders aren't finding information through these channels, you can bet your next commission check that they have an army of influencers that are doing just that.

Connect Call Mechanics

Finally, you're probably wondering how a connect call works. The short answer is that this will be different for every business, but the following are insights I've learned myself over the years and try to teach others.

How Long Should the Connect Call Last?

The connect call should be no more than 10 to 20 minutes, depending on the types of products and services your business sells and whether those products/services are an "aspirin" or a "vitamin" (need to have vs. nice to have). Let me repeat myself—about 10 to 20 minutes. No more. You can go less than 10 to 20 minutes, but I would be surprised if you ever feel like you're running out of things to ask your prospect in a 10-minute window. Remember, if you're working in a sales environment that requires you to work more than a handful of deals per year to make your numbers, you need to systematically work through a relatively large volume of prospects daily (likely, anywhere from 20 to 40 per day or more). Every minute you spend with one prospect is one minute less you are able to spend with another. In addition, keeping the call to 10 to 20 minutes is designed to leave the prospect wanting more. Remember, you likely caught them out of the blue. You are there to add value, establish some trust, and leave them wanting more. Get off the call.

What Specific Pieces of Information Should I Be Gathering during the Connect Call?

I have thought about this question many, many times over. How much information is too much? Which pieces of information are the right ones to gather? Should it vary from rep to rep or not? Why or why not? My first piece of advice is that, whatever you decide, it should be decided at the SVP, VP/ director, or segment level; in other words, the information should be standardized. This allows an organization to scale faster and provide consistent training to all, from all levels, organization-wide. At a minimum, make sure you finish your connect calls with this type of information:

♦ A firm grasp of whether the prospect has a compelling reason to change, and what that reason is

♦ A clear understanding of why that compelling reason carries urgency with it; in other words, "Why now?"

♦ The role this person plays in a purchasing decision, which may not be obvious from their LinkedIn profile alone

♦ As firm an understanding as possible as to whether the person and their company is in an active buying process or not (this is sometimes very difficult to gauge)

♦ Any other pertinent information correlated with your ability to help a prospect address their compelling reason to change (but not more than what you can gather in 10 minutes or less)

Is It Okay to Speak with a Lower-Level Employee, or Non-Decision-Maker?

Short answer: Yes. You're going to have to start somewhere. Does this mean you should talk to an intern or an executive assistant? Probably not, but not "definitely not." You must remember that the decision-maker is rarely the one doing all the research on how to solve his or her problem. They often delegate that information gathering to lower level team members and you should earn their trust to move up the decision-making ladder. Make these people your champions and so long as they involve the true decision-makers and give you access to those decision-makers, they will be your best friends.

SHOULD I PUSH BACK OR EVER "GO NEGATIVE" DURING THE CONNECT CALL?

Absolutely. During the connect call, you should always be leading with how you can help your prospect. And if you're running the connect call properly, you probably have many positioning statements designed to tease out those pain points your business helps prospects solve.

For example, inside of HubSpot's Agency Partner Team, we would often use a positioning statement that sounded something like this: "Typically, when I speak with an agency like yours, they express concerns over their clients coming to them asking for services they don't provide. As a result, they have often had to refer that business away. To what extent has that happened to you and your team?"

The idea here is to use the positioning statement to find a vein that opens a broader conversation. I recommend anywhere from three to four positioning statements that could open those longer conversations. As you go through these statements, if you find that your prospect isn't reacting to anything, it's probably time to go "negative." However, the way in which you go negative matters, and it's delicate. Here's how I would recommend delivering it as simply, professionally, and politely as possible: "Well, it sounds like everything is going pretty well and there's no reason to change the way you're doing things now. Would you agree or did I miss something?"

The beauty in going negative is that the outcome is binary. It's a yes-or-no outcome. This is a time where you want to ask a closed-ended question instead of an open-ended one. After delivering the "going negative" lines, the prospect will either agree with you, in which case you've accurately assessed the situation and saved yourself and the prospect time, or the prospect will tell you that you're wrong and will instantly reveal exactly what they're looking for help with and why it's so urgent to address now. In other words, they'll end up selling you on why you should keep talking with them!

How Do I Wrap Up the Connect Call and Transition into the Next Steps?

Again, this will depend on the specific sales process that your organization has laid out and that you should be following; however, there are a few things I recommend assuming the prospect is a fit relative to your personas and is active in the buyer's journey. First, do not ask whether a prospect would like to have another call with you. Tell them. At this point, you know better than they do as to whether they're a company you can help, so say so. As you wrap up, I would use something like this: "I know you weren't expecting my call today, but I appreciate you taking some time to connect. Based on [*compelling reason to change*] and [*why it's important to address now*], we might be able to help you; however, I need to learn more about your business. I have my calendar open now for [*whatever time*] tomorrow morning. Is that available for you too?" I cannot reiterate how crucial this step is—not only on the connect call, but for every step of the sales process. One of the most common mistakes sales reps make—and one of the easiest to fix—is not having a clear next step decided on and a corresponding date on which that next step will happen.

Done successfully, you'll have booked the next call. So, you're probably wondering . . . "What happens next?"

Chapter 5

Explore

*How to Properly Explore a Buyer's Goals
and Challenges*

If you miss everything else you read in this book, do not miss
this chapter. The exploratory call is *the* most important part
of running an effective inside, and arguably outside, sales
process. It is where all the rapport is truly built. It is where
trust codifies. It is where your prospect will begin feeling
slightly uncomfortable, which will resolve as you work with
them to build the solution to their goals or challenges.

The simplest way I can explain this step in the inbound
sales process is that you are continuing to learn exactly what
"current state" your prospect has found herself or himself in. It
is your job to understand that current state as thoroughly as
possible. Once you do, it is also your job to help them understand how to get to their future, desired state. This is another
core component of being an effective inbound seller—staying
in control, but consulting your prospect to the point where they
feel empowered to make the right decisions.

Observing and running sales processes for the better part of
the past decade, I have noticed this step tends to be one rarely
missed, but poorly executed by most salespeople. Average
sales reps will start this call or meeting off by recapping what

they learned on the first call or interaction, if they even had one, and will go into information gathering mode.

They will go about asking questions around data points like budget, authority, need, and timeline (BANT). This is referred to as the classic BANT approach to selling that so many sales professionals use. Let me tell you something—*BANT alone is dead*. While these pieces of information are in fact important and helpful, they are inadequate and insufficient to drive a sale forward. They also do little, if anything, to empower the prospect. They are virtually wholly sales-rep focused, not customer-focused. And this is exactly where inbound selling flips the traditional model on its head—it is designed to transform the way traditional salespeople sell to match the way that modern buyers buy, which, in part, means focusing on the buyer's needs first and the seller's needs second

In addition, most sales reps I've listened to without training will go about gathering these facts—or what they think are facts—without challenging or questioning what they hear. For example, if a prospect tells the sales rep that their sales goal for the year is an additional $X million in revenue, the average rep might respond by saying, "Wow, that's great." He or she may then proceed to ask more questions about what the company has done historically, and what they feel like they have done well or poorly to achieve those results along the way.

On the other hand, a great salesperson realizes that asking a question will simply get you an answer, not necessarily the truth. So, a highly skilled salesperson will not just take information that he or she is given at face value. They will dig deeper, far deeper, to understand the truth behind what is being said. For example, if a great rep hears that their prospect's sales goal is $5 million in revenue, they will start asking questions such as "How did you arrive at that goal? Is that a goal that's a nice to have number, or need to have number? Who was involved in coming up with that goal? What's the upside (or downside) to missing, meeting, or exceeding that goal? Can you 'war game' with me for a minute or two?"

I liken this line of questioning to the identification and diagnosis of a health issue. The connect call (covered in the previous chapter) is like a patient (the prospect) calling the doctor's office main line (you, or a BDR/SDR) to explain that they have a health issue they're concerned about. In this analogy, the exploratory call is the prospect's first visit to the doctor's office. The doctor (you) will start by reviewing the medical record (from the Identify phase we discussed, as well as the small amount of information we gathered in the Connect stage), and will likely continue the dialogue by asking an open-ended question like "So, can you tell me more about what's been going on?"

The patient (prospect) then proceeds to describe the issue while the doctor (you) takes notes and starts thinking about follow-up questions to accurately diagnose a situation. The patient (prospect) might point to her or his "knee" as the source of concern. The doctor (you) might then might ask how long "the knee" has been hurting for, whether she hurt the knee in the past, what type of pain she's experiencing, the extent of the pain (1 for barely; 10 for unbearable), and so on and so forth. The doctor (you) may even then go on to touch "the knee," continuing to ask things like "Does it hurt here? How about here? And when I go behind 'the knee,' here, too?"

They're diagnosing the situation. Even then, after the initial appointment, the doctor (you) may not know what the true issue is. He or she might recommend the patient (prospect) get an X-ray, a CAT scan, blood work, and so on—some sort of a diagnostic test that will provide both the patient (prospect) and the doctor (you) a clearer picture of the true nature of the problem. This is what we call the Advise step in the inbound sales process, which I will cover in the following chapter. For now, I'll continue to focus on what that initial "doctor's appointment" conversation sounds like, and how you can start crafting questions that will help you continue to pursue your "inbound selling PhD."

Getting in the Right Frame of Mind

As you start to think about what exactly your company does and how it helps its customers, take the mindset that when you're speaking with a prospect you should treat them very similarly to a good friend starting a business, or at least a friend that is working in another job now and facing a challenge.

Would you express deep interest? Probably. Would you ask a few follow-up questions to understand the true nature of what was going on? Most likely. Would you ask about other people your friend works with, what they're like, and how they drive (or do not drive) decisions forward? Yes. *So why then do we as sales reps tend to shy away from these more "personal" questions when engaging with prospects?* Why do we not sell the way we interact with virtually all other humans, every single day of our lives?

My hypothesis is that either sales reps don't feel comfortable asking these questions, or they simply do not know how to ask these questions. Or worse, someone trained them to ask only a specific set of scripted questions. My focus here will be on the "how" of asking these questions as opposed to developing the courage. Your level of comfort will be derived through role play with other team members, your manager, an outside sales coach, and through real life practice.

Exploratory Call Question Examples, in Context

At HubSpot, the purpose of our sales and marketing software is to help businesses grow and scale faster, at a lower cost. Specifically, we help our customers do this by giving them the technology and education they need to grow their website traffic, increase the volume of leads generated through their website, improve the quality of communications they have with those leads as they approach being ready for a sales conversation, and turn customers into promoters of their business over the long term. In short—it's a front-office software platform to help businesses grow faster. Therefore, the questions I'm going to give you as examples from the exploratory calls that I've had relate back to these sorts of business objectives. As you read these questions, think about the core business problems that your company solves or alleviates for its customers and start jotting down some questions that would be relevant for the types of buyers you engage.

While we incorporate the BANT approach in qualification, we also often use a framework called "GPCTCI": Goals, Plans, Challenges, Timeline, Consequences, and Implications. Again, we use this framework to understand, as completely as possible, what the prospect's current world looks like, what their future world looks like, what's standing in their way to get to the future state, their level of desire to fix those challenges, and how urgent it truly is to fix those problems.

Here's a loose framework for the generalized types of questions you might be asking someone during the Explore phase of the inbound sales process. Again, don't just drag and drop these questions into your own calls. Customize. Make them better.

Business (and Sometimes, Personal) Goals
- What's at the top of your priority list for the rest of this year?
  - Put another way, if I were to look at the to-do list on your desk right now, what would I see?
- How did those things make it to the top of the list?
- How do those priorities relate back to revenue (or cost reduction, risk reduction, efficiency, etc.)?
- Are there specific revenue goals you're working toward or being held accountable to?
- How did you, or the business, arrive at those goals?
- Would you say that those goals are nice to have or need to have?

- If they're nice to have, is there a need to have number?
- Why is that number a need to have?

Plans to Achieve Your Goals or Overcome Challenges

- How long have you been working on getting to that goal?
- What have you tried to achieve this goal or overcome this challenge in the past?
- What worked well? What didn't work so well? Why do you think that is?
- What's your plan now to achieve the goals we discussed?
- Who else is working on it?
- Is this at the top of their priority list?
  - If it isn't, what is?
  - What needs to get done before this becomes a top priority?
- How much time do you think they'll need to effectively work on these goals with you?
- Given their current workload, do you think they'll be able to do this and keep up with their other responsibilities?
- Do you think you'll need to hire someone to bear the workload? Why or why not?

Challenges Inhibiting You from Achieving Goals

- How long have you been working on this goal?
- Why do you think it has been challenging to get there?
- Do you think you'll need to change your approach to get to your goals?
- What do you anticipate being easy, or difficult, as you make that adjustment?
- Is there anyone you work with that would be a "likely candidate" for derailing this work?
- Why do you think they would derail this work?
- What specifically do you think you'll need to do differently to achieve your goals?
- Are there any parts of your plan that you're unsure about? In other words, are there specific areas of your plan that you think you'll need extra help with?

Timeline to Start Working Toward, as Well as Achieve, Stated Goals

♦ What's your timeline to achieve these goals?

♦ How did you come up with that timeline?

♦ If it took you an additional month, three months, six months, to get there, is that okay?

♦ Why is delaying okay, or not?

♦ To get to those goals on time, when do you think you need to start the work?

♦ How did you decide that?

♦ What needs to happen before you (and your team, if applicable), can start working on the project goals?

Consequences and Implications if Goals Are Exceeded or Missed

♦ If you exceed these goals, by say 20%, what happens? Dream out loud with me.

♦ If you miss these goals, by say 20%, what happens? Scenario-plan out loud with me.

If you're selling into a small business or even mid-market company, these types of questions will get you and your prospect fairly far along together. However, if you're selling into enterprise businesses (at least 1,000 employees or more), there are some additional questions you'll want to weave in along the way. Here are some examples:

ENTERPRISE-LEVEL INFORMATION GATHERING EXAMPLES

♦ To what extent does your company have a pre-defined process in place for purchasing goods/services?

♦ Which steps are involved in that process?

♦ Which individuals are involved in that process?

♦ Which functions are required to "sign off" on any purchases?

♦ Are there different processes in place for different purchase amounts? If yes, tell me more about that.

♦ When do team members from procurement, finance, legal, security, etc., get involved?

- Have you worked with businesses like ours or used products/services like ours in the past? If you have, how did that purchasing process work? What would you have liked to do differently, given the chance?
- *[If you're in an incumbent sale situation and the incumbent is no longer present]* Can you give me a sense, maybe on a scale of 1 to 10, what it was like working with that company? *[The point of asking this question is to see whether the business feels "burned" by businesses like yours in the past].*
- What do you anticipate as the primary hurdle in making some of the changes we've discussed? Why do you feel that way?
- Who do you anticipate as the primary or secondary hurdle in making some of the changes we've discussed? What sort of relationship would you say you have with that individual?

Of course, I realize that all these questions are in fact generalized and not specific to any type of business, per se. So, to help you better visualize and understand what this looks like in practice, I'll share another powerful part of my Inbound Selling Playbook, called the recap letter. HubSpot does not necessarily endorse this in the inbound sales methodology, but I used this tool as an integral part of my sales process as a rep and coached my reps to do this as a manager, so I feel it's worth sharing.

Exploratory Call Follow Through: The Power of a Recap Letter

As you read through this, I want you to remember that the sales process has at least as much to do with what you do off the phone as you do on the phone. In addition, the sales process is dynamic. So even if you nailed the exploratory call, you need to keep nailing everything throughout the entire process. One meeting or conversation never makes a perfect sales process.

This is like interviewing for a job. When you interview, there are a series of steps you go through. You're competing against an employer's alternatives. You are trying to make yourself stand out in such a way that you stand head and shoulders above the rest of the candidates as the obvious choice to your prospective employer. So why then would we forget these simple concepts when it comes to selling for our company?

As I mentioned, one of the steps I employed as a sales rep was called the recap letter, or champion's letter. The key difference between a recap letter and a champion's letter is that the recap is typically used earlier in the sales process and usually posits more questions as an addition to the exploratory call itself, whereas the champion's letter does not ask questions and is delivered as a final presentation to an influencer, or CEO, when very final decision making draws near.

In short, I hope this example helps bring the loose "exploratory call script" together. Again, I cannot reinforce how important it is to *not* sound scripted; instead, the more you express genuine curiosity, the better you will do on exploratory calls and meetings. In addition, by taking the time to write these recap letters, you're doing three things:

1. First, you're giving yourself a chance to fully digest and understand the conversation you had with your prospect. Your notes are not going to look this tight during your conversation. Taking time to go back to your notes a few hours after your call will give you a fresh perspective on what you learned and will give you a better sense of how much or how little you really captured.

2. Second, by writing and recapping your understanding of the goals and challenges your prospect is facing,

you're going to make them feel like they have been heard. Again, this is a chance to delight your prospects before they become customers. A light goes off in their head that reinforces the notion that they're being listened to and understood. This rarely, rarely happens. In contrast, when I'm on the buyer's side of the equation, I usually get follow-up emails from sales reps that say something like *"Brian, Thanks so much for talking today. It was great and I really look forward to showing you how our technology can help HubSpot improve XYZ."* This kind of follow-up makes me feel like a total cog in the wheel. And I get that I am in fact most likely one of many opportunities a rep is working. I've been on their side of the phone. I get it. But because I understand the world from their perspective, this is even more reason not to follow the typical sales rep's path. Take the extra 30 to 60 minutes required to recap your conversation; it will pay off. The deals that I did this for closed at twice the rate when compared to those for which I didn't.

3. Third, by writing this recap, you're giving yourself a chance to ask insightful follow-up questions. This is okay! Another stumbling point that I've seen reps run into is following a sales process too closely. So, they ultimately end up on two sides of a spectrum—either they follow no sales process at all because they do not know any better; or they follow the process so blindly that they lose sight of what they're doing and why they're doing it. Our Chief Sales Officer at HubSpot, Hunter Madeley, uses an analogy that I really like for situations like this. He says (and I'm paraphrasing), *"We want to give our reps the playbook that takes them down to the 20, 15, or even 10-yard line. What they do from there is up to them. That's where innovation happens and where we want them to have complete*

control. The rest is on us as sales leaders to craft for them and with them." By giving yourself the opportunity to ask insightful follow-up questions, you're helping yourself, but you're also helping your prospect think more about the issues they shared with you, and you're driving the conversation forward by simply asking follow-up questions to cover in the next call.

To bring this to life for you, here's an example of a recap letter I wrote relatively early in my sales career.

Subject: Recap of Goals and Challenges for [BUSINESS NAME]
Hi Judy,

Before our call tomorrow I thought it would be helpful to share my notes with you from yesterday.

Below, I have summarized my understanding of your goals and challenges. In addition, I had a few follow-up questions, which are included throughout different sections. Feel free to respond directly to those questions, or we can go over them tomorrow.

If there's anything else I can do between now and tomorrow please let me know.

I. BACKGROUND ON [BUSINESS NAME]

♦ *[BUSINESS NAME] was founded in 2001—the agency grew to about $3.5MM revenue in 2007–2008, has condensed back down to about $1MM revenue since.*

(*continued*)

(continued)

♦ *The agency works with a wide variety of client types—especially city, state, municipal, and retail clients—but also has a very strong presence in the manufacturing industry.*

♦ *Your core services include marketing strategy, branding, graphic design, communications, some content creation, email marketing, and social media management.*

Follow-up Question:

♦ *Is that right? I feel like I may be a bit off here. You currently have six full-time employees on staff.*

II. SALES AND BUSINESS DEVELOPMENT GOALS

♦ *You're currently trying to regrow the business and get back to 2007–2008 revenue levels of $3.5MM+ (back up from $1MM current).*

♦ *You also want to move to a retainer-based model to smooth overall cash and improve revenue predictability.*

♦ *The ideal client would represent a retainer of ~$10K/month, or $120K/year.*

♦ *You're currently looking for ways in which to make your clients more successful with their overall marketing work.*

♦ *Your long-term goal is to sell the business and exit within five to seven years.*

Follow-up Questions:

♦ *Is getting back to $3.5MM a nice to have or a need to have goal?*

♦ *If it isn't a need to have, is there a minimum revenue goal you need to hit before the end of this year?*

♦ *Where do you want to be in terms of revenue when you're preparing to sell the business?*

PLANS TO ACHIEVE YOUR GOALS

Client Targets

♦ *You would like to be more effective in targeting and servicing larger clients.*

♦ *You have struggled to be efficient with clients that generate less than $500K, often times because they have an insufficient budget or are too sensitive to budget.*

♦ *An ideal target generates between $5–$10MM/ year—they are large enough to support a marketing budget, but still too small to have a proper marketing team internally.*

Follow-up Questions:

♦ *What types of challenges do you think your ideal prospects are facing?*

♦ *What types of questions do they typically ask?*

♦ *How does [BUSINESS NAME] address their challenges?*

Internal Marketing

♦ *You're currently working with a video production company to boost your search engine rankings.*

♦ *In addition, another agency handles overall SEO work for [BUSINESS NAME].*

♦ *You also use Cooler Email to run email campaigns.*

(continued)

(*continued*)

Follow-up Questions:

- *What else are you doing for your own marketing and lead generation? What am I missing?*
- *Is anyone dedicated to marketing internally?*
- *Who runs the email marketing campaigns? Who oversees the SEO and video development work internally?*
- *I saw that you have a blog but haven't posted in awhile. Who contributes? Is there any reason it has slowed down?*

Sales/Lead Generation

- *You and Ann own business development responsibilities.*
- *The majority of your work is focused on getting out to networking events and generating word of mouth referrals.*
- *You also have a strong presence on Facebook and LinkedIn but not so much with Twitter.*

Follow-up Questions:

- *Who is managing Facebook and LinkedIn now? Why do you think it has been successful?*
- *Do you feel like what you're doing for lead generation now is working? Is it sufficient?*

CHALLENGES YOU'RE CURRENTLY FACING

- *Cash Flow: Cash flow is inconsistent.*
- *Client Payment: Too many clients are on net 30 terms. You struggle less to get new clients on board, but more with getting them to pay you on time (or at all).*
- *Expectation Setting: You need to find a better way to set expectations up front with clients in order to*

> · *avoid late payment, as well as "scope creep" on the work you're doing (driving down profitability).*
> ◆ *Sales and Business Development: You feel like you're not engaging the right types of clients.*
>
> **Follow-up Question:**
> ◆ *Am I missing anything here? Or am I misstating any of the challenges we talked about?*
>
> **TIMELINE, CONSEQUENCES, IMPLICATIONS**
> ◆ *Improving your own lead pipeline and shifting to a retainer-based model is a current priority because you want to be able to exit the business in five to seven years.*
>
> **Follow-up Question:**
> ◆ *Are there any consequences or implications (positive or negative) of missing or exceeding your goals? I don't remember talking about any.*

If you've still not bought into the value of a recap letter after running the exploratory call, take a quick look through the top 10 factors that most separate winners from losers in a B2B sales process from the RAIN Group (see Figure 5.1).[1]

Reviewing the list, what stands out is that all of the top five factors can be practiced through a combination of both the exploratory call and the recap letter.

- ◆ Educated me with new ideas or perspectives—exploratory call
- ◆ Collaborated with me—exploratory call and recap letter
- ◆ Persuaded me we would achieve results—exploratory call and recap letter

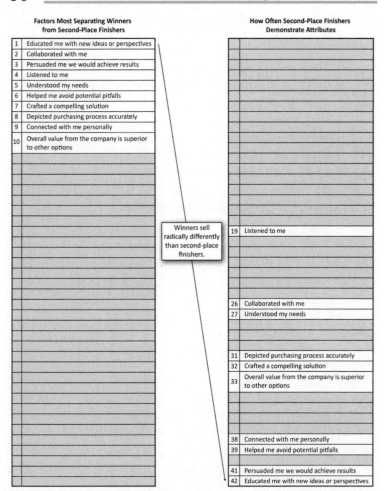

Factors Most Separating Winners from Second-Place Finishers		How Often Second-Place Finishers Demonstrate Attributes
1	Educated me with new ideas or perspectives	
2	Collaborated with me	
3	Persuaded me we would achieve results	
4	Listened to me	
5	Understood my needs	
6	Helped me avoid potential pitfalls	
7	Crafted a compelling solution	
8	Depicted purchasing process accurately	
9	Connected with me personally	
10	Overall value from the company is superior to other options	

Winners sell radically differently than second-place finishers.

19	Listened to me
26	Collaborated with me
27	Understood my needs
31	Depicted purchasing process accurately
32	Crafted a compelling solution
33	Overall value from the company is superior to other options
38	Connected with me personally
39	Helped me avoid potential pitfalls
41	Persuaded me we would achieve results
42	Educated me with new ideas or perspectives

FIGURE 5.1 Top 10 Factors Separating Winners from Losers in a B2B Sales Process

Source: What Sales Winners Do Differently (RAIN Group, 2013). Reproduced with permission.

- ◆ Listened to me—can be achieved on the exploratory call but proved with the recap letter
- ◆ Understood my needs—again, can be achieved subjectively on the exploratory call but demonstrated with the recap letter

Chapter 6

Advise

How to Advise a Buyer on Whether or Not Your Solution Addresses Their Needs

A t this point you may be thinking, "What? Another step? Why am I not asking for the sale, moving to a demo, or sending a proposal?" The answer—because that's exactly what your prospects are expecting you to do.

Most sales professionals, myself included, have a little demon that they battle. That demon is called "happy ears." The happy ears come out when the prospect is telling you everything you want to hear. The prospect is excited. They tell you they've bought in to working with you and your business. They tell you they absolutely need to implement your company's products or services *now* because it's the best thing invented since sliced bread. In fact, this was even proved to be a very real phenomenon by Gong.io in a blog post titled "Here's Why Your "Sure Thing" Deal Didn't Close (and What to Do Next Time)," by Chris Orlob.

But that's just the thing—they are only one person, and rarely are purchasing decisions made unilaterally. In fact, research shows that on average at least five people are involved in any B2B buying process across a wide variety of functions—from the C-Suite to Sales to Procurement to IT to Legal to Finance, and so on. And this number is only expected to rise by

2020, according to research from the Corporate Executive Board.[1]

Therefore, we need to "know thy prospect." If you had multiple decision-makers or influencers on a previous call, that's great, but it's not sufficient. Consider this in relation to a first date—do you really think that after someone responds to you on Tinder, Match.com, or whichever platform you want to use as an example here, and you go out on one date that goes well, they're ready to commit to a relationship with you? Of course they're not!

Similarly, circling back to our doctor-patient analogy from an earlier chapter, do you think that a doctor is going to be able to prescribe a treatment or medication solely on the basis of a handful of questions you answered? Again, N-O! Instead, during that initial visit, your doctor may have asked you to get some blood work done, to go for X-rays, or some other type of diagnostic test. He or she needed more data and more time to understand what the proper prescription might be. You as a sales rep must also take these steps if you have any chance of earning your prospect's trust and commitment.

Despite knowing this practical wisdom, many reps' happy ears inevitably perk up, at which point they get seduced into going for the close. This is not only the wrong approach it is bound to turn your would-be buyer off. You're not fully understanding them, appreciating their company's purchasing process, or getting their full commitment to implementing a plan you discussed. This is exactly why we need to layer in the "Advise" step, or Goal Setting and Prescription, as it was once referred to at HubSpot.

While this may seem repetitive, putting this additional step in between qualification (the "Explore" stage) and close is designed to provide further buying validation because it's a cooling off and reflection period for everyone. Your prospect may have been "hot" the first time you spoke with him or her, but are they still feeling that urgency and excitement the second time around? That's what the Advise step is there for—to confirm that urgency, that excitement, and the verbal commitment to an implementation plan. In essence, it serves as a joint-planning call. You and your prospect should be using this time to revisit and refine the plan you all discussed during the exploratory call, which you should both believe will help the prospect overcome his or her challenges and achieve their goals.

Whenever I have performed a goal setting call (advise call), there's a "hit list" that I use to make sure I have everything nailed and to ensure that there's a clear go/no-go by the end of the call.

Here's how it works:

First, I start by reconfirming the goals, plans, challenges, timeline, and consequences/implications I discussed with the prospect during the exploratory call. I am going to ask them deeper questions in each of these topic areas (again, another reason why the recap letter is a powerful tool—it's the lion's share of your checklist for the advise/goal setting call).

In an ideal world, we have already uncovered and developed a deep understanding of our prospects goals, plans, challenges, and timeline. In addition, in an ideal world, we have uncovered both the positive and negative consequences, or implications, of making—or not making—a change to the way their business operates. Yet to assume that all sales processes run ideally is, of course, a fool's errand. We know that conversations can be sloppy. They get sidetracked, cut short, run long. Even though we may have talked for anywhere from 30 to 90 minutes, we may not have truly uncovered all the relevant information we needed to uncover. And that's OK. It's the point of the Advise step in the inbound selling process.

How to Assess How Much You Really Know about Your Prospect before the Advise Step

One way to self-assess the quality of the information you uncovered during the exploratory call, aside from writing the recap letter itself, is to use a simple rating system that has a meaning behind it. When I was a sales rep on HubSpot's Agency Partner Team, we used a simple 1-2-3 rating system that accompanied each bucket of information we discussed with a prospect.

Rating a bucket of information as Level 1 meant that we uncovered some information, but it wasn't quantifiable. Rating a bucket as Level 2 meant that we uncovered quantifiable information about a goal, a plan, or a challenge but didn't understand the significance behind the numbers. Finally, Level 3 meant that we not only had a quantifiable response to the bucket, but we also had a full understanding of *why* something had to happen within a certain timeline and usually had a consequence associated with it. If your business uses the concept of *exit criteria* to move a deal from one stage to the next, these concepts are somewhat like exit criteria. Following are example statements with associated rating levels to help you understand this system and start thinking about how you would apply this to your own company's sales process.

Rating Levels in Action (Example): For the "Goals" Bucket of our Exploratory Call

Level 1 example: "We need to grow our website traffic and generate more leads for our sales team."

Level 2 example: "We need to grow our website traffic by 25% and generate at least 50 net new leads per month."

Level 3 example: "We need to grow our website traffic by 25% and generate at least 50 net new leads per month. If we don't start seeing these results within the next three months, we will miss our sales goal for the coming year and will need to lay off at least 25% of our sales and services team members."

Do you see the difference? Do you also see the progression across all three rating levels? If you don't, go back and read them again. Slowly.

Again, I realize that this information relates back to a software company whose business purpose is to help a marketing team generate more website traffic and convert more leads for its sales team to work more consistently; however, the concepts themselves still apply to any business. Your company helps its customers solve a specific problem or set of problems through its products, services, or solutions. In case you don't feel comfortable clearly articulating what those business challenges are for your prospects and how your business addresses them, start thinking about them now.

As this pertains to the Advise stage of the sales conversation, remember: you are not a robot. You are not a machine. The odds of you getting a perfect Level 3 for all your qualification buckets are slim to none. That's why it's so important to write out your recap letter for your prospect and revisit all of these areas during the advise/goal setting conversation. This is at least as much for your prospect as it is for you. By the time the goal setting conversation happens, you probably will have started to formulate some solutions and the way you want to articulate them to your prospect, but you also probably still need some more information from them.

Preparing for the Advise Conversation

Before your goal setting conversation ever happens, it's paramount to write out all the questions you need to ask to get your level of understanding as close to Level 3 as realistically possible. It's probably not going to be perfect, but the more preparation you do ahead of time, the more valuable the conversation will be to you and your prospect. And that matters. In doing this, you will be far more capable of articulating the specific ways in which your company can help your prospect solve the issues or challenges they're facing. In turn, this builds deeper and deeper trust with your prospect, which ultimately increases the odds that they'll choose to do business with you instead of a competitor.

Second, once you fully confirm these components, dig deeper into understanding who your prospect may have shared information with at their company. One of the most classic mistakes I see my newer team members make is not fully understanding who influences a purchasing decision. Based on research from CEB, we know that in any typical B2B sale, about five people are involved in moving a purchase forward or shutting it down.[2] Often, we think that if we're talking to a business owner, that's the only person we need to speak with because that person is the boss. If they're the boss, doesn't what that person says, go? Sometimes, but not always. Not everyone operates their business unilaterally, and leveraging the knowledge of sales research, we know that rarely is any purchasing decision unilateral.

Even for those of you selling to a small business, if you're speaking with, for example, a husband and wife team that operate a business, you better make sure you have a full understanding of how those two make purchasing decisions. For example, if your prospect says, "Oh, I handle the finances, and my husband handles everything else," don't take their word for it. Get deeper confirmation that the other half of the equation has fully bought into the plan you're formulating before progressing the conversation. The earlier this is uncovered and addressed, the less likely you're going to hear "Well, Brian, this is all great, but we need to take this offline, run it by the team, and get back to you," when you thought you were approaching the close.

Third, make sure you dig deeply into a plan a prospect has discussed or shared with you to overcome their challenges and to achieve their goals. The key objective you should be aiming at is to both challenge the prospect on whether their plan will help them achieve their goals and to co-create the plan with them. I have always found it far more effective to get something done when someone has complete buy-in to a plan rather than to prescribe one to them that they may or may not fully agree to implement. After all, people are resistant to what they hear but believe what they say—and therefore, co-creating a plan with your prospect is critical.

For example, if we need to get multiple people involved in implementation, I'm going to ask about who those people are, by name, what they're working on now, and what needs to be accomplished before that person has enough bandwidth to dedicate time to an implementation now or later. I need to understand what other priorities that person may or may not have to fully grasp the reality behind an implementation timeline the prospect and I have "agreed" to in theory. In addition, I need to fully understand whether the plan the prospect and I are devising has been discussed with the people who are going to be doing the work or going through any sort of training. If those people are not fully on board with the plan, it will get blocked and a contract will never get signed.

Here's an example of the tools I use and the questions I would ask during the goal setting call as an account executive, based on the example worksheet shown in Figure 6.1.

PART 1: GOALS, PLANS, CHALLENGES, AND TIMELINE

What We Know
- ◆ $30,000 in recurring revenue now
- ◆ Wants to add three customers paying $3,000 to $6,000 per month in the next 12 months

Example Tie-Down Questions
- ◆ This means an additional $9,000 to $18,000 per month in the next 12 months, correct?
- ◆ How did you come up with these numbers?
- ◆ When you hit them, what will you do with that additional revenue?

GPCT

Structure your own Goals, Plan, Challenges, and Timeline

4	Goals	Our goal is to increase the revenue of monthly re-occurring marketing services by 60% in the next 12 months. We would need an additional 3 customers per month paying $3,000 to $6,000 to achieve this.
5	Plans	Retention of our current clients is a must to achieve this. We have improved our workflow processes and project management system. We are working on efficiency measures. We have also launched our new website and are currently working on some high level calls to action.
6	Challenges	Our challenge is that there's a lot of skepticism around our industry. We are good at what we do and we provide valuable and honest consultation for our clients.
7	Timeline	We want to get started and hit the 3 new accounts mark latest by September 2015.
8	Additional Notes on GPCT	**No Additional Notes**

FIGURE 6.1 HubSpot Goal Setting Diagnostic Tool (Goals, Challenges, Timeline)—Part 1

Source: Courtesy of HubSpot.

FIGURE 6.2 HubSpot Goal Setting Diagnostic Tool—Part 2

Source: Courtesy of HubSpot.

♦ *Final Tie-Down Question*: If you miss them, and you can't do these things, does that really make that much of a negative impact on the business?

PART 2: PLANS TO ACHIEVE SALES AND MARKETING GOALS

Advise on Retention

♦ It seems like retention is a very high priority. Are you struggling with retention at all now?
♦ Do you anticipate this being an issue?
♦ Why do you anticipate this being an issue?
♦ Where do clients push back on your work?
♦ Why have clients ended up leaving in the past?

Advise on Internal Marketing (see Figure 6.2)

Example Tie-Down Questions

♦ Who is doing marketing work for you now?
♦ Are they responsible for generating leads for the business?
♦ Are you comfortable that the flow of leads you're getting now will get you to those goals?
♦ Do you want them to be?
♦ Is that part of the plan going forward?
♦ *Final Tie-Down Question*: Have they bought into this plan? If we were to train them and help them improve your overall marketing for lead gen, is that something you'd want our help with?

Advise on Sales (see Figure 6.3)

Example Tie-Down Questions

♦ Who's responsible for sales now?
♦ Do you feel confident that they'll hit your sales numbers if they don't make any changes to what they currently do?

Get Started		Processes	
GPCT		*Help us estimate your agency's current financial health.*	
Business Evaluation			
• Attract	103	Do you have a list of questions you use to qualify whether a lead is a good fit for you and whether you can help them?	**Yes**
• Convert			
• Close			
• Analyze	104	Do you have a process for helping your prospects set reasonable goals and a plan to help achieve them?	**Yes**
• Services			
Agency Finances			
• Revenue	105	Do you use a customer relationship management system to track sales activity, performance, and forecast revenue?	**Yes**
• Profitability			
• Growth			
• Processes	106	Additional Notes on Business Processes	**No Additional Notes**
Funnel Analysis			

FIGURE 6.3 HubSpot Goal Setting Diagnostic Tool—Part 3
Source: Courtesy of HubSpot.

♦ If not, what changes do you think they need to make?
♦ Do you plan on selling to new customers or existing customers?
♦ What does your lead/opp pipeline look like right now?
♦ What's your average sales cycle (months)?
♦ *Final Tie-Down Question* (if they need to make changes): Are you and your team open to changing a few things about the way you sell? If we were to show you a better way to sell services retainers, is that also something you'd want our help with?

Advise on Services (see Figure 6.4)

Example Tie-Down Questions
♦ How is your service team structured now?
♦ How does your team deliver all of the services you offer now? How many tools do they use?
♦ Are they comfortable with using all of those different tools now?
♦ How do they do reporting?
♦ Does anything feel manual right now?

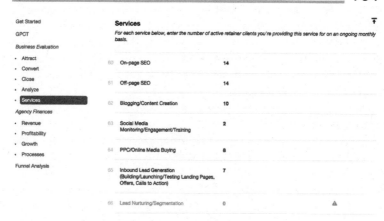

	Services		〒
Get Started			
GPCT	For each service below, enter the number of active retainer clients you're providing this service for on an ongoing monthly basis.		
Business Evaluation			
• Attract	60 On-page SEO	14	
• Convert			
• Close	61 Off-page SEO	14	
• Analyze			
• **Services**	62 Blogging/Content Creation	10	
Agency Finances			
• Revenue	63 Social Media Monitoring/Engagement/Training	2	
• Profitability			
• Growth	64 PPC/Online Media Buying	8	
• Processes			
Funnel Analysis	65 Inbound Lead Generation (Building/Launching/Testing Landing Pages, Offers, Calls to Action)	7	
	66 Lead Nurturing/Segmentation	0	▲

FIGURE 6.4 HubSpot Goal Setting Diagnostic Tool—Part 4
Source: Courtesy of HubSpot.

- How many hours do you spend per month on reporting per client?
- Are there any metrics clients ask to see that you struggle to show? Why?
- Are there any metrics that clients are not asking for but that you'd like to show? Why?
- If you were able to expand your services—into email, automation, lead nurturing, sales enablement, revenue reporting, and so on—do you think you could bill more for your services and attract larger clients?
- Is that also part of your plan?
- Who would be responsible for learning those new services?
- *Final Tie-Down Question:* Do you want our help training those team members in learning new services?

Advise on Pricing and Packaging (see Figure 6.5)

Example Tie-Down Questions
- Are you comfortable with how your services are priced and packaged now?

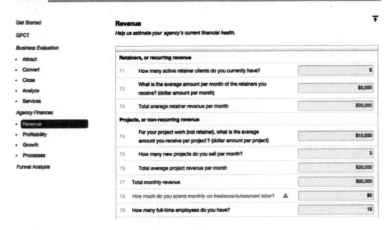

FIGURE 6.5 HubSpot Goal Setting Diagnostic Tool—Part 5
Source: Courtesy of HubSpot.

♦ If not, what changes do you think you need to make?
♦ *Final Tie-Down Question*: If we were to show you the right way to price and package these services, is that something you'd want our help with?

Advise on Hiring (see Figure 6.6)

Example Tie-Down Questions
♦ Do you have any hiring plans for the next 6 to 12 months?
♦ Which roles are you hiring for?
♦ How did you decide that those were the most pressing roles you need to hire for?
♦ *Final Tie-Down Question*: Is this an area you'd like our help with as well?

I do fully realize and appreciate that the previous example is very, very specific not only to the software platform I was selling but also the Partner Program I was advocating for as a manager and account executive. However, it does not mean that a similar process should not be developed or could not be

GPCT   ⊤

Structure your own Goals, Plan, Challenges, and Timeline

4	Goals	**Our goal is to increase the revenue of monthly re-occurring marketing services by 60% in the next 12 months. We would need an additional 3 customers per month paying $3,000 to $6,000 to achieve this.**
5	Plans	**Retention of our current clients is a must to achieve this. We have improved our workflow processes and project management system. We are working on efficiency measures. We have also launched our new website and are currently working on some high level calls to action.**
6	Challenges	**Our challenge is that there's a lot of skepticism around our industry. We are good at what we do and we provide valuable and honest consultation for our clients.**
7	Timeline	**We want to get started and hit the 3 new accounts mark latest by September 2015.**
8	Additional Notes on GPCT	**No Additional Notes**

FIGURE 6.6 HubSpot Goal Setting Diagnostic Tool (Plans)—Part 6
Source: Courtesy of HubSpot.

developed, for your company. You have also probably realized that we have a strong sales enablement team that builds online questionnaires for our prospects to complete, and for our sales team to review with them. Let me tell you it was not always this way. Excel spreadsheets, Google Sheets, or Google Forms can work just as well.

You do not necessarily need an online tool and questionnaire to go through a goal setting call effectively. If you think you and your company can develop a similar rubric to add value to the sales exploration process, I absolutely encourage you to do so. However, if you cannot, I would argue that the value in the goal setting call (Advise stage of the inbound sales methodology) is not in fact the tool I used to run or guide the call; instead, it was all in the clarifying questions I was asking my prospects and the subsequent plan we co-created to overcome their challenges and to achieve their goals.

In other words, you do not need a visual crutch or aid to add an immense amount of value to your prospects during a goal setting conversation. The preparation and questions you review—alone—will be a huge step in the right direction. It's also important to keep in mind that the "weight" of your sales process will probably be, to some extent, directly correlated with the size of the sale. If you sell a product for $50 a month, the sales process should be a lightweight and fast one, whereas if your average sales price is $100,000 a year, it's likely going to be a heavy and long one. Even as I reflect on my own sales process to this day, it was likely far too heavy for the average price we were selling—around $10,000 to $15,000 a year.

Switching gears back to the flow of the goal setting call itself—beyond having a firm grasp on the composition of the company's implementation team (users), you also need to fully understand what their buying process looks like. At a minimum, I need to know who will be involved, what types of factors they take into consideration when buying a product or service, and whether they have purchased products or services like mine in the past. If they have, what type of buying experience did they have? Did they have a good one and were they satisfied with implementation? If not, what went wrong? Did they feel burned? Do I already have a bad reputation because of a poor purchasing experience another sales rep somewhere else left for me to clean up? Knowing these pieces of information up front will help me tailor my approach with a specific prospective customer through their entire purchasing process.

To properly conclude the Advise step, you'll actually need to advise. This begins by succinctly summarizing everything you and your prospect have discussed, advising on where specifically you believe your business can help them, and concludes with you explicitly asking your prospect whether they're committed to making the changes required to achieve their goals. Some people refer to this as the "soft close." In part, it's referred to as "soft" because you're not asking the prospect to sign a contract right then and there. Instead, you're asking them if there's any reason at all they *wouldn't* proceed with implementing the plan you've developed together, which you've both agreed will help them achieve their goals or overcome their challenges.

But before moving to this soft close, which is not in fact "closing" but is instead the natural conclusion to the Advise step, I always gut check one last thing—and that's the degree of variance in the plan the prospect and I have discussed relative to how they have tried to attack the same goals and challenges in the past. Is it really that different? Why or why not? Putting myself in a CFO's or CEO's shoes, I need to see concrete evidence that the new plan my team members are presenting has credibility in its divergence from previous plans that failed. I will also need some level of concrete evidence that the proposed approach has worked for other companies and provides an ROI greater than the required investment in making a change (or total cost of ownership). Provided I have these pieces of knowledge, it's time to move to *the soft close.*

CONCLUDING THE ADVISE STEP: THE SOFT CLOSE

I cannot reinforce how important it is to wait to present the soft close, or what was taught to me as *the inoffensive close* (credited to Dave Kurlan in *Baseline Selling*), until you have gathered a deep understanding of the business you're working with as well as the key players and decision-making steps involved. If you don't have this information, the attempt at a soft close will fall flat on its face.

As previously mentioned, the purpose of the soft close is to further establish the prospect's commitment to moving forward and to ensure you, as the inbound seller, have not missed any steps in the qualifying process. In addition, of course, it's designed to ensure you don't waste your time putting together a contract, a presentation, a demo, a proposal, or a price quote that will ultimately get shuffled away under a pile of other emails or paperwork. If you've never used a soft close, here's the exact script for one that I use. Of course, you should tailor this to your own business; it is not a "drag and drop" script.

[As you move into the closing 10 minutes of the goal setting (Advise) call . . .]

> **You:** [Prospect Name], I know we've covered a lot during today's call, as well as in our prior conversation. I appreciate the time you took to discuss your goals and challenges in depth and to co-create a new plan to address these goals and challenges. At this point, do you feel like I have a deep understanding of your business and what you're trying to achieve?
>
> **Prospect:** Yes. Yes, I do. [Again, this is what they should say if you've done your job well.]
>
> **You:** Okay, good. And do you feel confident that the plan we've co-created is going to help you and your team overcome the challenges we discussed and get you to your goals?
>
> **Prospect:** Yes. I do.
>
> **You:** Okay. Are you sure there's nothing we missed?
>
> **Prospect:** No, we didn't miss anything.
>
> **You:** Good, I'm glad to hear that. Out of curiosity, is there by any chance an alternative plan that you and I haven't discussed—that you feel equally confident in—to overcome these challenges and get to these goals? [Note: You would be shocked at how many

times a prospect or company has a second hidden agenda that they haven't brought you in on, so it's a best practice to check. You should have enough rapport by now to have the right to ask about an alternative.]

PROSPECT: No, there's no other plan.

You: Okay. So, at this point, we typically put a contract together to do a more formal demonstration of [insert your product/solution here]. Assuming [product/proposal/etc.] meets your expectations, is there any reason you won't be ready to start working together?

In this final question, you may get an objection that sounds something like, "Well, we haven't talked about price yet." If you get this objection, you should have covered price already. Don't make that mistake again. If, however, you need to deal with it in the moment, I would recommend asking the last question in the inoffensive close sequence again, prefaced with, *"Pricing aside (or off the table) . . . is there any reason you won't be ready to start working together after [demo/ presentation, etc.]?*

Chapter 7

Closing and Negotiating

Drawing from my own experience, I know that a lot of sales reps have room for improvement when it comes to asking for someone's business. For example, at the end of an exploration or sales process, I often hear sales reps say something like "Well, what did you think? What are the next steps?" This often ends with the prospect saying something like "It was great but I need to circle back with the team and see where we go from here." Then the chase begins.

But what if the chase didn't have to happen? Or what if it happened less often? What would you do with all that extra time? To help all sales reps and sales leaders continuously learn and improve a wide variety of sales skills, I'll start by sharing this "greatest hits" list of closing techniques. Pete Caputa and Danielle Herzberg taught me these techniques, so connect with them on LinkedIn or Twitter and say thanks.

The Inoffensive Close[1]
This is the closing technique I discussed at great length in the previous chapter. To the best of my knowledge, this closing technique first appeared in Dave Kurlan's book *Baseline Selling*. Dave does not necessarily endorse what I say here, nor does he necessarily support the accuracy of this description,

but I certainly want to give credit where it's due—and thanks, for that matter, as this was a tried and true method I've used throughout my career. This approach, as outlined next, was specifically taught to me while I was a rep at HubSpot under Dannie Herzberg and Pete Caputa.

As you approach the final stages of your exploration or sales process, use this line of questioning to assert your knowledge, confirm it with your prospect, and prescribe the next step. This technique works particularly well with the "S" (Steadiness) and "D" (Dominance) personality types from the DiSC behavioral assessment.[2]

First, recap what you know: *"Based on everything we discussed, I see four major areas that we can help with through a partnership: Improve your internal marketing, consolidate tool sets and improve efficiency, expand services down the funnel and grow retainer revenue, and do some training with your team. Is there anything that I missed, or that you would add to that list?"*

If your prospect says no, ask the following four questions in order:

1. At this point, do you feel like I have a good understanding of your business and what you're trying to achieve?
2. Do you believe the plan we've laid out will get you to those goals?
3. Do you have any alternative plan to achieve those goals?
4. Assuming the [demo, presentation, etc.] meets your expectations, do you want our help by partnering together?

The last question secures the close, without coming off as aggressive or pushy.

The "1 to 10" Technique

If you've already gone through the HubSpot inbound sales methodology training, this technique isn't going to be a surprise to you. But if you haven't, I'll share this nugget of wisdom now.

The "1 to 10" closing technique works particularly well with prospects that fit the "I" (Influence) and "C" (Conscientiousness) personalities from DiSC. It is designed to help the prospect fully weigh the benefits and drawbacks of working with you. As you approach the conclusion to your exploration or sales process with a prospect, ask the following question:

> *"So, [Prospect Name] on a scale of 1 to 10—1 being 'we should end the call' and 10 being 'sign me up now'—where would you say we are at this point?"*

If the prospect says 6 or lower, something went wrong in the earlier stages of the sales process, and you need to go back and retrace your steps. However, if they name a number higher than 6, follow up with this question:

> *"Huh, I'm surprised you chose a number that high. Why did you choose it?"*

By asking the prospect to explain their high number, you're prompting them to elaborate on the *benefits* of working with you. After the prospect finishes listing benefits, you'll then want to get them to outline their concerns so you can address them. Here's how:

> *"Huh, those sound like some pretty strong reasons to work together [paraphrase their reasons back to them]. But now I'm even more confused. Based on the reasons you gave, why isn't your number a 10?"*

At this point, the prospect will start giving you their objections or concerns, and you should take time to walk through them thoughtfully and carefully. After all outstanding concerns or objections have been addressed, ask:

"Now that we've talked through your hesitations, has your number changed at all?"

If their number is still not a 10, deliver the following line:

"Okay, I understand you still have some hesitations. Earlier you shared [benefits of working with you]. Then you also shared [objection]. Comparing the benefits and risks side by side, do you think the benefits of working together outweigh the risks?"

If they say yes, proceed to final contract terms. If they say no, the deal goes to closed-lost. Either way, you've brought the process to a close.

The Perfect Close

This last one isn't really a technique, but rather a way for you to determine how well you ran your sales process. If at the end of a goal setting call, presentation, or demo—before you say anything—the prospect says, "Okay, how do we get started?" that is the sign you have run a flawless (or near flawless) sales process. The prospect is so bought in that they are asking *you* how to buy.

How do you get to this point? Continuously focusing on all the stages that precede the closing call and executing with precision every step along the way. Strive to build a sales process so strong that you never even need to use a closing technique, and your quota will be within your reach month after month.

Facing Reality: Closing and Negotiating Are Similar, but Not the Same

The equivalent of an ocean sits between knowing how to close and doing it with proficiency. To be an effective inbound seller, you also need to know how to handle resistance, objections, and points of negotiation that you will almost inevitably face along the way. While you can teach anyone to employ the closing strategies outlined here, teaching negotiation is far more difficult because there are simply so many ways in which a business may try to negotiate with you.

Unfortunately, I see many reps struggle significantly with this step, often unnecessarily. They just aren't provided the coaching they need to finish off a sales negotiation properly. It's not their fault. They're used to seeing negotiation tactics that revolve around outdated or vague methods. To confirm this, I did a Google search for *"How to negotiate a sales deal"* (see Figure 7.1).[3]

FIGURE 7.1 Google Search Results for "How to Negotiate a Sales Deal"

I'll save you the extra reading time and share the highlights of what I reviewed here. Keep in mind that I don't necessarily endorse or agree with these techniques, I'm simply providing a synopsis of what I found in the first page of the search results. My commentary on the extent to which I agree or disagree with each piece of advice is contained in the sections that follow.

CONVENTIONAL SALES WISDOM #1: "NEVER NEGOTIATE WITH INFLUENCERS"

This one is pretty straightforward, but you don't always have complete access to decision-makers during the entire sales process. In addition, there is typically more than one decision-maker in any given sale, and the influencer may be one of them. I agree that negotiating with the influencer or influencers *alone* is probably not going to drive the results you're looking for, but the influencer can be your champion to tip you off or coach you on what types of points need to be addressed in the contract signing process. Don't count this person (or these people) out.

Disagree.

CONVENTIONAL SALES WISDOM #2: "NEVER BE THE FIRST TO MAKE AN OFFER"

I also understand where this one is coming from, but I could make an equally valid argument as to why you should be the first one to make an offer. If you know you need to negotiate around price to get a deal done, then in my opinion you're better off setting the range—referred to as "anchoring"—rather than letting the prospect set the range. The key to this is starting the range low, using dollar figures or percentages—whichever appears more powerful or substantial. For example, a 5% discount may sound like a slap in the face, but if you're negotiating a sale for a $100,000 per year product that equates to $5,000 annually—an amount that carries far more weight than 5%—then you're in a much better negotiating position.

Disagree.

CONVENTIONAL SALES WISDOM #3: "UNDERSTAND THE DIFFERENCE BETWEEN A TRADE-OFF AND A CONCESSION"

This is probably my *most* favorite point raised by the team at InsightSquared. In effect, they define a trade-off as a give/get. For example, if you offer a 5% discount then the prospect will sign their contract two weeks earlier than planned. However, a concession is one-sided. In the same scenario, the prospect may demand a 5% discount or threaten to take their business elsewhere. Because the prospect is viewing you as a commodity in this second scenario, either something went wrong in the sales process itself, or you're potentially dealing with a poor-fit potential new customer that's going to cause a lot more problems down the line. Walk away from people like this.[4]

 Agree.

CONVENTIONAL SALES WISDOM #4: "NEVER START NEGOTIATING TOO EARLY"

Again, a straightforward principle. No further commentary needed. Negotiations should not begin until you have finished the soft close or inoffensive close. In other words, don't start negotiating unless you have an agreement, at least in principle.

 Agree.

CONVENTIONAL SALES WISDOM #5: "OFFER THE ULTIMATE PACKAGE EARLY"

When I read this piece of advice, I think I understood where the author was coming from, but it was poorly communicated. In effect, I think they were trying to talk about how much the product or service with the most bells and whistles costs. However, *I completely disagree* with proposing a product, service, or solution that your prospect does not need. This not only completely undermines your credibility as a rep, it sets your prospect up for a poor experience. The "ultimate" product may offer functionality or services that the prospect simply does not need or is not at the point where they'll truly get more value out of it than what they paid. In addition, because of the oversell, you're setting the services or account management teams at your company up for disaster. Do *not* do it.

Instead, when it comes time to recommend the product or service, inbound sellers recommend the *right* product or service for their prospect and make sure they can stand behind why they're recommending it. Your prospect will appreciate this even if it's more than they were expecting to pay. Setting a range early in conversations will also help. For example, quoting a price by starting with the highest and moving back down to the lowest reverses the psychology of price negotiation. It gets "better and better" (to the prospect) as you go because you're coming down to lower and lower levels of pricing instead of causing them heartburn by going in the opposite direction.

Totally disagree.

CONVENTIONAL SALES WISDOM #6: "BE PREPARED TO WALK AWAY AND USE SILENCE TO YOUR ADVANTAGE"

The last tactic that stood out to me revolved around walking away, or just saying nothing at all. However, these two methods are completely different (walking away from a sale vs. staying in the sale and using silence). Let's take a closer look at each.

First, being prepared *to walk away* from a negotiation and *delaying a close* are completely different notions, yet many reps tend to conflate the two. For example, you might offer a concession on price or payment terms *if* the prospect can sign the contract by a certain date or time. Observing this specific method anecdotally over the years, I'd say that about half the time the contract is signed within the stated timeframe, half the time it is not. When it is not, the prospect usually comes back asking for "just one more extension." At this point, the sales rep has a bit of egg on his or her face, but is almost always able to get the contract window renewed. This is just a reflection of an incomplete sales process or a misunderstanding of the steps the prospect needed to go through to purchase your company's products or services. It is *your* job to help them navigate their own buying process. Unless you are a rep with only a few months' experience, you should have seen many transactions successfully completed and you should be better suited to coach your prospect through their own buying process even though you don't even work at their company!

Walking away from a deal, on the other hand, is a completely different idea. It doesn't mean you're going to walk away entirely if a prospect missed signing your contract within an allotted timeframe. Instead, this may mean making a judgment call somewhere in the sales process that the prospect is not a good fit for your company's business model. Unfortunately for the seller and the prospect, this sometimes happens very, very late in the sales process during negotiation. A common example of this may include a prospect that drags you and your company through an abnormally long due diligence process, asks to redline terms and conditions beyond standard contract adjustments, or demands abnormally extended security or background tests or checks.

A proficient inbound seller should be able to flag these potential issues early, but we're human and don't always nail this. It's also easier for me to say it while quietly writing out these ideas rather than being under the live fire of a negotiation on the last day of a month or quarter. Regardless, once these issues are identified—namely, that the customers' demands fall outside 90 to 99% of all other prospective customer requests—a rep should be prepared to walk away from a deal entirely. Assuming a company is compensating its reps the right way, then the rep should have every incentive to walk away from the deal because it will be problematic not just for the company, but also their wallet.

Lastly, using silence is far more powerful than most reps may give it credit for. As one of my favorite team members and leaders at HubSpot once said, "Silence is power." Specifically, and again anecdotally, I have experienced and observed many prospects literally talk themselves into—and then straight out of—tough demands during a negotiation, solely because the sales rep has not responded whatsoever. While I'm not a psychological expert by any stretch of the imagination, I suspect it is related to the simple fact that few people are truly comfortable with silence. So, my advice here is simple—when in doubt, stay silent. Hit your mute button on your phone if you just can't keep your mouth shut. Watch at least ten to twenty seconds count off on the phone and I guarantee you'll re-establish control of the conversation.

While there exist a handful of negotiation tactics in these articles, none of them truly addresses the next logical follow up question, which is *"That's all great, but* how *do I do it? How do I become an effective negotiator?"* Here's how.

How to Negotiate

First, when entering a negotiation, take price off the table completely. Meaning, confirm with your prospect that the contract itself is the absolute last thing standing between your business and their business working together. You might ask, "Price and contract aside, is there any reason at all you or your team are not ready to start working with us?"

By isolating price or terms as the sole factor standing between you and doing business with the prospect, you ensure that nothing else has been missed and that if you come to agreement on terms then the next step is to get a contract signed. Many times, when I observe reps begin a negotiation, they don't triple check that price or terms are in fact the very last factor or factors standing in between them and the close.

Second, when you bring price or terms back to the table, make sure you quote the price or terms *exactly* as they should be quoted. For example, if your company bills annually, then state the price as an annual figure. Breaking it up into a monthly or quarterly equivalent, without ever being asked, does not provide you with any leverage whatsoever and makes your prospect feel deceived.

Third, when you quote price and terms, do not negotiate with yourself. In other words, state the price and terms—and the price and terms—alone. Hit mute on your phone, or, if in person, zip it. Learn to be comfortable with silence. It is a source of power. If you start discussing anything other than the exact price or terms your prospect—if he or she is a good negotiator—will let you keep going until you offer them a deal that they did not even ask for.

Fourth, when your prospect reacts to the price or terms, they may push back—stand your ground. For example, the prospect may say, "Wow, that's expensive." Or "Is that the best you can do?" Or "Is that just your list price?" If and when they do this, both your verbal and non-verbal response will set the tone for the rest of the conversation. Do not, under any circumstances, emotionally react to their pushback. Instead, counter with a question like "What do you mean?" or "Expensive compared to . . . what?" or "Why do you ask?" or "Huh, I've never been asked that before."

They'll likely either drop it or they'll push you to start negotiating. When they do this, reconfirm that price or terms are in fact the very last thing standing between the two of you and that if you come to terms the next steps are to move forward.

Fifth, use optionality. Instead of pushing your prospect for a price, consider giving them one of two paths related to the investment. The question that I've had the most success with is the following: *"Is this a budget issue, or a cash flow issue?"* (I also realize there are some companies out there that have a "zero-discounting" policy. If you work for one of them, amen. I love that. If you don't, keep reading.) By presenting the negotiation like this, you're setting yourself up for a trade-off, not a concession. In other words, you're asking them to prioritize whether the entire amount (budget) is the issue, or the frequency with which payments are made (cash flow) is the issue. This is where your leverage begins. If they come back with budget or come back with cash flow, follow them down this path but reinforce what the standard price or billing term is. Once that's done, ask, "What did you have in mind?" Or "Where do we need to be to make this a no-brainer?" Whatever they state, acknowledge it, but don't agree to it. Assess whether this is within your acceptable range of negotiation and if it is, make the trade-off and close the deal. If not, keep going.

What Happens If the Prospect Doesn't Agree to One of the Two Paths Presented?

Often, especially with smaller businesses, you'll hear an additional objection to the "budget versus cash flow" question; specifically, the prospect's answer will be: "It's both."

Early in my sales career I used to take complete offense to this. I would push back by telling someone they were overreaching, or by telling them to try and answer the question again. You may also feel that guttural reaction—that your prospect is being greedy. Fight against it. Put yourself in the prospect's shoes. They may very well see all the value that your company provides, but they should also be looking out for their own company and trying to minimize the investment the best they can.

If you do in fact get to this point in the negotiation, you may want to circle back to the question you asked originally and reinforce/reconfirm that price and terms are in fact the only things holding the prospect back. You may also want to reframe the question by asking, "If XYZ were free, would we already have you on board?"

If at this point your prospect has confirmed that price is the only thing standing in their way, yet they require multiple concessions, ask them to paint their ideal world for you. Usually, once someone does this, you may be surprised how little they ask for. If they ask for a lot, then you have a baseline for negotiation. My tried and true method is generally splitting the difference of the request because it is in most people's nature to come to consensus.

If, however, they still do not agree to move forward, you may be in the unfortunate situation where you ran a less than ideal sales process, missed something along the way, and may in fact need to walk away from the deal. If they're being this unreasonable now, how many other things are going to be issues? Some people just aren't capable of being helped, or being helped for a price that makes sense on both sides of the table. Alternatively, you may try the "1 to 10" closing technique outlined earlier to get to the heart of the prospect's remaining concerns.

Last, if you're dealing with a slightly large or very large company, remember—you may have more of an upper hand than you think during the negotiation process. If they do not have a worthwhile alternative (which, in the case of large companies is usually doing nothing, a very real alternative) to moving forward with the plan you helped them build by investing in your company's services, then they have little to no negotiating leverage. This is often referred to as the BATNA— Best Alternative to Negotiated Agreement. That's not to say that you should use this unfairly to your advantage and put the strength of the relationship at risk, but you should have faith that if you have truly helped a prospect think through their goals and challenges and laid out a clear plan to address those challenges in the timeline required, then they should have every desire to partner with your business. Don't be afraid to remind them of that either in case they forgot!

Part 3

How to Lead Inbound Sellers: Reflections for the Front-Line Sales Manager

Chapter 8

The First-Time Sales Rep-to-Manager Survival Guide

Why sales management? I must have been asked this question at least a dozen times as I was transitioning out of the individual contributor role and into my first full-time leadership role at HubSpot. Many questioned my intentions. "Why would you give up the freedom? Why give up the autonomy? Why give up the flexible work schedule? Can't you make more money as an individual rep?" they all asked. They were right that you sacrifice most of these things when you decide to make the move from individual contributor to leader. But there was a lot more that I felt I had to offer and new ways in which I thought I could help the company grow.

For example, I enjoyed seeing others succeed as reps more than I enjoyed my own success as a rep. The excitement in selling a big deal or significantly outperforming started to fade after a few years. Sure, getting contracts signed, helping people, and being a top performer all gave me a rush, but the intense selling "high" itself had worn off.

I also felt a sense of obligation to give back to the company that had given me the opportunity to grow my career and learn a whole new skill set. When they hired me as a rep, I had virtually zero sales experience. They bet on me and their bet paid off. They had trained me in exactly how to do what we do. I listened and learned, and the results followed. In my mind, it was time to pay back that debt or, perhaps, pay it forward.

Finally, I truly believed that the impact I could have on the overall business would be far greater as a leader than it ever could be as an individual rep. In a good year, I sold about three quarters of a million in new revenue, which for a company selling products mostly to small and midsize businesses with an average sale price of about $10,000 was significant. Was that meaningful? Sure, it was. But what more could I really do than just that? What types of results could I drive if I multiplied my reach 5 times, 10 times, or more, I wondered. What would it mean to help others learn what I had learned and help them assert a firm control over their destiny the way that I had? The answer was that I would have an opportunity to make a disproportionate impact on growth and scale if I decided to lead, and so I did.

I'm sharing this reflection because I so often hear people say that they want to get into a leadership role because "It's the next logical step" in their career. I don't generally believe in bad answers to questions, but this is an exception—this is definitively a bad answer.

If you're an individual contributor now, and that's your reason for taking on a leadership role, I can tell you that you are almost certainly not going to enjoy sales management and leadership. I would encourage you to rethink your reasons and don't even contemplate a move until you have concrete, personally meaningful motivations to make the switch. If you're a director or VP of sales and you hear that from one of your team members, push them hard to dig deeper for answers. That said, if you are considering making the switch and pursuing a sales leadership position, the following are some reflections and advice I hope prove to be useful.

So, You Think You Want to Be a Sales Manager?

(Adapted from a blog post I wrote titled "7 Things I Wish I Knew before Becoming a Sales Manager," https://blog .hubspot.com/sales/things-i-wish-i-knew-before-becoming- a-sales-manager.)

If you're an individual top-performing contributor in your sales organization and you're thinking of applying for a sales manager role, I'd like to give you a bit of a reality check first. Here are some disturbing data points that may make you think twice about taking on that front-line manager role:

◆ Sales managers cannot control 83% of the metrics they're held accountable to.[1]

◆ A full two-thirds of all salespeople miss their quota.[2]

◆ Over half of all salespeople close at less than 40%.[3]

◆ Forty percent of salespeople can't understand customer pain.[4]

◆ Only 46% of reps feel their pipeline is accurate.[5]

◆ Almost half of all sales teams don't have a playbook.[6]

◆ Only 52% of salespeople can access key players and decision-makers.[7]

If after you read those stats I haven't talked you out of applying for a sales manager position, I'd like to share some reflections I made after my first year in the role. In my opinion, these are the seven things you should know that I personally wish I knew before I started.

1. Forecasting Should Be the Least of Your Worries

For some reason, I thought that accurately forecasting and reporting my team's numbers was going to be a huge obstacle to overcome. It wasn't. If you're an organized person you'll be just fine. The most difficult thing to get used to is managing a funnel of 8 to 10 times the number of opportunities you're used to managing as an individual.

	A	B	C	D	E	F
1	Team Member	Opp Name	Deal Value ($MRR)	Close Date	Stage	Next Step
2	RACH	Acme Paper	$280	10/1/2015	Closed Won	10/1 - Closed Won
3	RACH	Acme Valves	$250	10/1/2015	Closed Won	10/1 - Closed Won
4	JILL	Acme Agriculture	$544	10/1/2015	Closed Won	10/1 - Closed Won
5	MITCH	Acme Education	$640	10/2/2015	Closed Won	10/2 - Closed Won
6	RACH	Acme Health	$640	10/2/2015	Closed Won	10/2 - Closed Won
7	BRIAN	Acme Accounting	$2,000	10/31/2015	Verbal	10/14 - Gave price; deciding between contracts
8	BRIAN	Acme Equipment	$1,350	10/31/2015	Verbal	10/14 - conversation with Eric tomorrow at 3pm – BC
9	BRIAN	Acme Manufacturing	$2,900	10/31/2015	Verbal	10/14 - conversation with Dylan tomorrow at 4:30pm – BC
10	RACH	Acme SEO Group	$950	10/31/2015	Verbal	10/6 - call scheduled for next week
11	RACH	Acme Technology	$850	10/31/2015	Verbal	10/6 - via Partner; losing control of sales process
12						

FIGURE 8.1   Example Manager Forecasting Spreadsheet

I did a few things to make sure I was forecasting accurately. First, I was always inspecting our CRM to ensure that my salespeople were logging their activities and updating stages on opportunities. Second, I asked my team members to tell me which deals were closable within the month, as well as the next 60 days. This way, I could pay closer attention to these deals, and coach on the opportunities that would have an impact on my team's attainment in the short and slightly longer term.

If you don't have all this information logged in your CRM, see Figure 8.1 for a spreadsheet template you can use.

Or better yet, if you don't have a CRM, use HubSpot's—it's free and is the CRM that sales reps will use (https://www .hubspot.com/products/crm). Reviewing this template in retrospect, I would also encourage you to add a column called "Missing Exit Criteria" or "Exit Criteria Required to Move Forward"—this should reflect the specific, predetermined action that the buyer must take to move from one sales stage to the next with your team member. Tracking this sort of information will enable you to become an effective and relevant coach for everyone.

2. SPEND MORE TIME RECRUITING IN THE BEGINNING THAN YOU THINK MAKES SENSE

If I could turn back the clock, I would have allocated more of my time to recruiting for my team. While I'm biased, I truly believe in Bill Belichick's (head coach for the New England Patriots) mantra that you must have the right people on the right bus to achieve great results.[8]

If you're not doing it already, I would highly recommend spending the equivalent of at least one day per week interviewing and meeting with potential new candidates for your team—regardless of whether you end up managing them directly.

Salespeople are famously focused on the next month or the next quarter. But rarely do reps worry about setting themselves up for success 9 or 12 months out. A sales manager, however, must think 12, or even 18 to 24, months ahead. Essentially, a sales manager must work on exceeding two numbers: their hiring targets and effectiveness as well as sales targets.

I'll paint this picture another way. There are two things a salesperson can screw up that causes them to miss their quota. The first is not putting enough opportunities into the top of the funnel. The second is spending too much time on deals that ultimately fall out of their funnel—closed-lost. The same thing can happen to a sales manager when it comes to recruiting. Continuously source enough candidates into your funnel and you'll reduce the chance of missing your number as a result. The key here is to build up a funnel of passive candidates that you can recruit when you're allowed to make that next hire or need to fill that open spot.

3. BUILDING TEAM UNITY REQUIRES ACTIVITIES OUTSIDE THE OFFICE

To me, managing a team of salespeople is like coaching a team of tennis players or golfers. Everyone may work on the same team, but they all have individual numbers. How do you create cohesion among the players?

If the team doesn't feel like they know everyone, they're unlikely to go that extra step to help one another. My advice: Make sure you spend time together and get to know one another. Plan team outings, team dinners, breakfasts, and

Figure 8.2 My Team Holiday Party (2014)

service events—anything that enables the team to get closer to one another outside of work will pay dividends. And remember, if you turn over 20% to 30% of your team in a year, that means your team is always changing. So, make sure you're planning events regularly. Each time you add a new team member, it's on you as the leader to rebuild cohesion and unity throughout that new team.

Figure 8.2 shows my team at our 2014 holiday potluck and Yankee Swap party.

4. You Will Have Far Less Time in Your Day Than You Might Think

Stepping out of "the funnel" and into the sales management role, I imagined that my days would be easier and less stressful than they were before. I wouldn't have an individual number on my head, and I would be responsible for coaching my team. I was dead wrong.

Instead of one number, I had 10. Instead of $500,000 for my quota, I had $4 million. Instead of having more time, I had less. My time was no longer my own, so I had to figure out which activities to prioritize quickly.

For me, the activities that I determined would have the biggest impact on performance fell into three buckets:

1. **Coaching:** What am I doing on a one-to-one basis to help my team members achieve their goals?
2. **Scaling:** What training can I facilitate that will help most of my team members perform better? Can I train them on things like selling skills, product knowledge, time saving tools, and so on?
3. **Recruiting:** What am I doing to continuously build the future success of the team?

Continuously evaluating myself against these three activities and whether everything I did lined up to them became the clearest and most effective way to maintain control over my time.

5. Define, Share, and Reinforce Your Sense of Higher Purpose Early

Most sales reps get a bad rap. Many believe that we're just out for money. Even in a 2016 HubSpot Survey—*The State of Inbound*[9]—respondents were asked to describe sales reps with one word; the most frequently occurring word was "pushy."

While I think there are certainly bad reps out there that fit the old "always be closing" profile, I don't think that most reps are like that. Instead, I think most reps want to understand why their work is meaningful and what purpose it serves. This thinking is backed by a variety of sales consultants and leaders, and exemplified well in an article by Next Level Sales Consulting.[10] Here's a quotation from the article that jumped out to me:

> *Salespeople who are intrinsically motivated are more fulfilled and financially successful than extrinsically motivated salespeople.*

Still don't believe me? There's some great research from Dave Kurlan and his team at Objective Management Group, such as:

> *In the old days (pre-2008), if salespeople were motivated, then they were probably motivated by money. According to data from Objective Management Group, 54% of salespeople were money-motivated during the 1990s and first half of the 2000s. Today, the data shows that no more than 27% of salespeople are what we now call extrinsically-motivated.*[11]

When moving into a sales manager role, you're also choosing to enter a leadership role. While anyone can be a leader—and hopefully you have a few on your team—leadership is a mandatory part of the sales management position. If you cannot define your team's or company's sense of purpose as a leader, you should work on it. Defining, sharing, and reinforcing that vision on a regular basis will constantly remind your team that the work they're doing matters.

If you're struggling to define your team's higher purpose, think deeply about why your company was formed in the first place. What challenge did it solve? What challenges do you solve now? How does this make your customers' lives better? How does this make the world a better place? Be specific! Quantify wherever you can. Salespeople love numbers. For example, here's an excerpt of an email I sent to my team on the vision and our purpose for working together (I sent this within the first 45 days of building my team in 2014):

SUBJECT: A Unifying Vision for Our Team as We Kick Off INBOUND 2014

Team,
    As we've been approaching INBOUND over the past few weeks, I've been doing a lot of thinking. Specifically,

I've been thinking about what exactly it is we're doing here and how it ties back to what HubSpot is working toward. How do we fit into this grand scheme?

During that time, I got the feeling that our team sometimes loses perspective on:

- "What exactly it is we do here"
- How that ties back to HubSpot's goals, mission, and vision as a business
- How our work impacts the Partners we work with (as well as THEIR customers)

As we head into INBOUND 2014, there's probably no better time to remind ourselves of the importance of our work and to not lose sight of these things. We can't lose sight. If we do, our work becomes void of purpose and we individually lose the sense of intrinsic motivation that should be propelling each of us forward every day. So, in the interest of keeping this short, I'll start with some high level perspective on where HubSpot is and then tie that directly into where we are.

In 2011, Halligan painted a high-level vision for Hub-Spot that I thought was elegantly simple, yet powerful:

> *"We're trying to build a multi-billion-dollar beast here in Boston. I don't know if we'll pull it off. We're trying to. We'd love this company to be like Hewlett-Packard, to be around for 100 years. We want to go go go."*
> —Brian Halligan, December 15, 2011

About 15 days later, HubSpot closed its books for the year and generated $29MM in revenue. In 2012, that number grew to $52MM. In 2013, to $77M. And if we

(continued)

(continued)

stick to the plan, in 2014 that will end up right around $100MM.

As I write this today, it's safe to say that HubSpot is taking the steps to become the billion-dollar business Brian, Dharmesh, and the rest of our executive team envisioned. But where does that leave us as a team?

How can we connect what we do each day back to those accomplishments? How do we paint our own picture to understand how what we do, day in and day out, rolls back up into the billion-dollar business that HubSpot's becoming?

Here's how I see it:

1. Our Team Makes a Massive and Material Impact on VAR Team Performance Every Month
   • Our team represents over X-Hundred of our Y-Thousand Partners—almost Z% of the Program itself (Z+% to be exact).
   • Not surprisingly, our team also carries over X% of the VAR Team's new sales quota (~K+ of ~K MRR).
   • 11 our of 41 US Team Members (which includes all BDRs, in case you were curious) = ~A% of the US Sales operation.
2. We Can Propel HubSpot Forward, or Stop It Dead In Its Tracks
   • Relative to the company, we represent just under X% of total new sales each month (*X+% to be exact*).
   • We also represent over $X-MM in annual, recurring software revenue for HubSpot, and that number is constantly growing (the sum of our collective Installed Base).

- By the time HubSpot becomes a billion-dollar machine, and as we add more team members, we will be a $X-MM+ operation (okay, I realize I'm reaching a bit here, but you can follow my logic).
- Therefore, our individual and collective performance month in and month out has a huge impact on HubSpot's overall ability to achieve its goals and realize its potential. If we slack off, HubSpot can and will suffer as a business.

3. Our Team Has, and Will Continue to Change, the Lives of Our Partners, Their Employees, Their Customers, and the Trajectory of Their Businesses

- That $X-MM revenue that our team generates every year translates into approximately $Y-MM in services revenue that we have helped our Partners generate over the years.
- Drilling down to each month, assuming we sell $X,000 of new MRR ($A-Z ARR), that translates to at least $E-F-MM in new services revenue each year for our Partners.
- In other words, we are on pace to be a ~$X-MM Operation by the end of this year and are projected to grow over Y% (net) year over year going forward
- And finally, as I hope you all saw in Pete's keynote speech last night, we were all collectively responsible for—on average—helping our Partners' businesses grow by A% in terms of head count and B% in revenue *in the past year alone.* That's a remarkable accomplishment to be truly proud of. This is yet another measurable way to know what we are doing works and matters.

(continued)

(*continued*)

So as we head into INBOUND this week, I want you all to take these numbers in. Internalize them. Let them sink in deep.

These are the badges of honor we all wear as Hub-Spotters. They are the collective reflection of your hard work, your hundredth prospecting attempt in a day, your 50th pipe review in a month, the 11th hour coaching call you had with a Partner before a deal closed, the final negotiation with a legal team, and the last dollar of MRR you close as you sprint collectively across the finish line to your manmade and self-set goals.

These are privileges we all enjoy. Privileges that have been afforded to few, but desired by many (you have no idea how deep the recruiting pipeline runs). They are the privileges we both individually and collectively realize each and every day because we are HubSpotters.

Here's to an amazing INBOUND 2014—carry these words and thoughts with you throughout the week and be proud to be part of the dream we're realizing together.

I'm excited to see all the amazing things we'll accomplish together this week, month, year, and beyond.

Onward and upward,

Sig

6. Your Direct Reports Are Not "Mini-Mes"

This is something I still sometimes struggle with to this day. The truth is many sales leaders will coach and manage their team the same way in which they were coached or liked to be coached. If you were direct and to the point with your manager, odds are that you'll want that from your reps, too.

However, the key here is not to follow the "Golden Rule" and "Treat others how you would want to be treated"; instead, follow the "Platinum Rule,"[12] and "Treat others how *they* want to be treated." I know this is easier said than done, but there are many training assessments out there to help. Get your company to give you the tools you need to succeed by enrolling in training sessions or classes on communication styles. I personally found the Intelligent.ly Manager Exchange Training[13] incredibly helpful in my early months as a manager. DiSC Assessments can also be a quick and effective way to understand your team members' communication styles and compare them to your own.

7. New Hire Onboarding Takes a Lot of Time and Is Key to Long-Term Success

In my first two months as a manager, I had to hire three new team members. It was a lot. Your new hires need just as much if not more of your mindshare compared to more tenured or, possibly, inherited reps. So, what is a new manager supposed to do?

First, make sure you clearly lay out expectations for your new hire, what milestones they should be hitting by when, and show them the resources and training you're going to provide to help get them there.

Second, consider asking your more tenured team members to be peer mentors. I find most people like paying mentorship forward because most great reps had a mentor that got them where they are today. This will ease some of the stress on your time.

Third, set up a regular cadence of small group coaching sessions. I would recommend twice per week as mandatory and twice per week as optional, allotting one hour for each of the four sessions. These are not designed to replace your one-on-ones—they should be in addition to that time.

Lastly, and I'll cover this later in this chapter—know the difference between training and coaching. Most managers conflate the two, leading to a manager regrettably transforming into a chief problem solver, which is not the role of a sales manager.

How to Convince Sales Leadership That You're Ready to Manage

Assuming I haven't dissuaded you from becoming a sales manager, your next step is to apply for the job. A big part of getting the job is showing that you're prepared. In most companies, if you're consistently overperforming, you can probably start to do some of the activities already mentioned. You can certainly help plan team outings, mentor new salespeople, help your manager source new candidates for the team, and maybe even improve team forecasting. You can even start to lead by sharing why sales and your company help you fulfill a higher purpose. I've always found that assuming the responsibility is the best way to earn it.

Finally, if your company offers training programs on preparing for management, or will even sponsor you to go to training sessions like Intelligent.ly, take full advantage of the opportunity. The more you can surround yourself with peers with similar ambitions and experiences, the more likely you'll be successful.

If your company does not offer any training programs, seek out mentors and start reading. Two books I'd highly recommend are *Suddenly in Charge* by Roberta Chutsky Matuson[14] and *Coaching Salespeople into Sales Champions* by Keith Rosen,[15] which I'll touch on in the following pages. Matuson does an excellent job providing foundational knowledge on managing both "down" and "up," while Rosen provides exceptionally actionable guidance on what it means to be an effective sales coach.

"Growing Up" as a Sales Leader

That was year 1 as a manager. But what about year 2 and beyond? Surely, there must have been more to being a sales manager than the simple seven steps I laid out in the previous pages. If you're feeling that way, I share your sentiment; it was in my second year and beyond that I felt like I had internalized deeper—and perhaps more existential—lessons in leadership, which you can start applying now and that I still apply today.

When I reflected on the second full year of managing, I wouldn't modify the reflections I just shared, but I would modify the way in which I presented those seven things. Specifically, I think the seven areas I highlighted were more akin to windows, doors, sheetrock, and HVAC if we're going with a house-building analogy. **What I think I truly left out was the foundation—which is exactly what I'm about to share**.

When I started managing, I was focused on:

1. Gaining trust from my team
2. Understanding what motivated each one of my team members to work with me and at the company
3. Ensuring I knew the fundamentals around sales forecasting
4. Identifying scale-based training initiatives
5. Managing my time effectively and efficiently
6. Building a team-wide vision and enabling team unity
7. Defining (and refining) the right way to onboard new team members

While all those endeavors were worthwhile, I realized that these things could and would constantly change. People came and went. Processes came and went. Sales targets and forecasting methods came and went. The market and competitive landscape evolved. Even the products and services we were (and are) selling evolved. It was all about *change*.

What I came to appreciate after going through an intense two-day coaching training with Keith Rosen, is that I wish I had known one "secret" ahead of time, far before I became a sales manager. **That secret? It's all about how to be a great**

coach, which enables you to be, or become, a great leader. I realized I had coaching all wrong.

I recognized that I viewed coaching as problem solving—which is more of a training and sometimes a motivation issue—when in fact I wasn't solving problems. Instead, I was only perpetuating a pattern of behavior that made my team more dependent on me, not less dependent.

I wrote off the reality that people needed to hear things five or more times before it sunk in to their base of knowledge. The way I knew this problem existed two years later is the simple fact that the same exact problems kept coming up repeatedly. Sure, they were in different forms, but they were all essentially the same. No matter how many group trainings, how many team meetings, or how many support resources I developed, the same issues were coming up repeatedly. Why?

The answer was simple: I had become the "chief problem solver," not a coach. I was not empowering my people to solve problems on their own and think critically. Instead, they were relying on me as their safety blanket.

Now, I believe that a great number of people struggle with this exact same issue, which was validated when my 40 or so peers in the room during Keith's training had this look on their face that said, "Oh, no. What have I done? I'm a chief problem solver, too!" If you feel this way, don't have a meltdown.

I further believe that most people get sales coaching wrong because they confuse the concepts of training and coaching. Let's break the two apart and give some definitions:

♦ **Training** can be loosely defined as the base of knowledge that an individual needs to consume and become educated on to do their job effectively.
♦ **Coaching,** however, is not about learning facts, how systems work, what the rules are, and so forth. Instead, coaching can be loosely defined as a communication

method that connects and engages someone in an **empowering** manner.

As further defined by Rosen, *"[Good coaching is] achieved through a process of ongoing, consistent interaction, observation and unconditional support in a safe and trusting environment that focuses on the unique and specific needs and talents of everyone in a way that facilitates long-term, positive change."*[16]

If You Want to Become a Better Coach—and in Turn, a Better Leader—Here's What to Do Next

First, I'd recommend you ask yourself whether your team members are asking you the same questions repeatedly. If they are, you probably have a training or motivation issue, which will need to be resolved either through more structured organizational knowledge transfer or through a "come to Jesus" style conversation about why that team member wants to work in the profession they've chosen, or at least on your team at your company.

Second, if you find that your team often comes to you with questions just looking for answers repeatedly—and you also find yourself jumping to give them the answers—then you most likely have a coaching issue on your hands. This suggested behavioral change clicked for me when I realized that as a sales rep I rarely ever jumped at the opportunity to give prospects answers and instead tried to empower them to answer their own questions. But as a manager, I threw that out the window almost immediately, and I was wrong. The easiest way to get back into this mindset is to think through how you would have acted as a sales rep with a prospect (assuming you took an inbound sales approach).

Finally, don't take this advice too literally. Use good judgment. In other words, there are going to be times that your reps do just need an answer and coaching isn't always appropriate.

For example, if your team member is in the middle of a call and slacks you or puts the call on mute to ask you a question—that's not the time for coaching.

Last, if you haven't checked out Keith Rosen's blog, http://keithrosen.com/blog, you certainly should. He's an amazing resource in this space.

Building on these concepts—if you had the same realization the way that I did about being a problem solver—are the following truths and advice about how to stop being a problem solver and start being a coach (i.e., a great leader).

TRUTH #1: FOR BETTER OR WORSE, YOUR SALES TEAM IS A REFLECTION OF YOU

When I heard this for the first time, it was a hard truth to accept. When I thought about all the wins and losses my team had experienced over the first two years, I felt good in some ways, worse in others. I felt great that I had helped many people reach their full potential. I felt great about bringing new people together. I felt great about helping individuals find meaning in their work, which ultimately helped them achieve significant personal life goals.

Conversely, I couldn't believe that I was the one causing the problem when I had team members ask me the same question for the tenth time. I was disappointed in myself for all the months that any team member missed their number. The list goes on.

The bottom line is that I realized I cannot care about anyone else's success more than they do, but I also needed to face the reality that any systemic problems on my team were more than likely caused by the way I was coaching or the absence thereof.

TRUTH #2: YOUR ROLE AS A LEADER IS NOT "CHIEF PROBLEM SOLVER"

When Keith Rosen presented this idea for the first time, I thought, "Duh, of course I'm not a chief problem solver." Then I gave it more serious consideration. How many times did someone come to me during the day? How many times had they pulled me into difficult situations, either a customer-facing or an internal challenge? How many times did they want me to solve their problems *for* them as opposed to them solving their problems on their own? The answer to these questions and more was "Too many."

The more I thought about this, the more I became disenchanted about what I thought management and leadership was, then quickly found the silver lining. I was surprised, as I reflected, to see that I had answered my team members' questions quickly and willingly when I taught them repeatedly that the way to more effectively sell is through open-ended questioning and digging deep into what a prospective customer was really asking them. Why hadn't I taken this same approach to management and leadership?

TRUTH #3: TO EFFECTIVELY COACH PEOPLE, YOU NEED TO ENROLL THEM AND MAKE YOUR INTENTIONS CLEAR

This is a somewhat opaque principle to grasp, but Keith did an excellent job teaching our sales leadership team how to do it well. In short, if any of the shortfalls I described previously resonate with you—being a chief problem solver or leading with solutions instead of questions when working with your team—then you probably need to rethink whether you're a coach.

If you're not a coach yet, but want to become one, the first thing you'll need to do is to enroll people into a new communication method. However, to do that effectively, you will need to clearly state your intentions. One of the best ways to do this, and it's nuanced so pay attention, is to sit down with your team members and explain why you're going to change your communication and preface it with "What I want for you . . ." Did you catch the nuance? It is critical that you use *"for* you" as opposed *"from* you" because the "for" implies that you have your team member's best interest in mind, whereas "from" implies you have your own agenda in mind.

Moreover, if you don't state your intention behind the change, your team members will default to fear. They'll think, "Am I on a PIP [performance improvement plan]?" or "What's going on at the exec level that's making my manager do this?" or "What's about to happen at the company that I don't know about?" By simply stating your intentions, you can remove this fear, and by simply changing the way you phrase your intentions, using "for" as opposed to "from," you will start getting better results as a coach almost immediately.

TRUTH #4: PEOPLE BELIEVE WHAT THEY SAY, YET ARE RESISTANT TO WHAT THEY HEAR

This is exactly why it's so important to be a good coach. If you are the one giving people answers all the time and telling them what to do, there is a much lower likelihood that a behavioral change will stick. Instead, if you coach someone into problem solving either for themselves—or at least *with* you—then they are the ones stating the solution, not you. Because they state the solution themselves, they are far more likely to believe it and, thus, act on it.

Getting a little existential: I'll pull a quote from the father of Taoism, Lao Tzu:

> *A leader is best when people barely know he exists, when his work is done, his aim fulfilled, they will say: we did it ourselves.*[17]

Here's a modified, hypothetical example of how this might play out: Your team member comes to you with an issue. Before anything else happens, you need to make sure you can give your team member your undivided attention. If you can't, tell them you can't, but ask them for a time that works for them because you really want to give your undivided attention. Once you do sit down, maybe open the conversation with "What's going on?"

They say that they're struggling to close a deal because a new decision-maker was introduced late in the sales process, and they want to know what you think they should do.

At this point, most sales managers will jump in and joyfully offer a solution. Why? Because we all want to be valued as human beings, and we're usually flattered that someone is looking for our amazingly "sage" wisdom on how to handle only the "most challenging" sales problems. This is the very first trap you must avoid. Instead, pivot the conversation back to your team member: *"Well, I'm happy to share my opinion on it [Brian], but since you're so much closer to the situation it sounds like you know best what the next step should be. So, what's your opinion on what we should do next?"*

If they resist this, consider backing up a few steps and ask a more open-ended question, *"Tell me more about the situation. What led up to the point you're at now?"*

After learning more about the situation, continue asking open-ended questions until you think your rep might be more receptive to the first question you asked, *"What's your opinion on the next step?"*

I didn't clarify this earlier, but I'll clarify it now—it is critical to use the word "opinion" because an opinion cannot be right or wrong. By using that single word, you eliminate the potential fear or self-doubt created when using a question like "What do you think the right thing to do here is?" It seems like such a simple question on the surface, but by merely injecting the word "opinion," you create a safer space for discussion.

At this point, if you have a very frustrated or difficult rep on your hands, they might just say, *"I don't know. That's why I'm asking you!"*

Most managers also fall into this trap—they think the jig is up and they succumb to their team member's frustration. But when someone says, "I don't know," it rarely means they don't know. Instead, it means: "Just give me the answer because I don't want to think for myself." Unless of course, this isn't a coaching issue, and is a knowledge gap—an example might be something more mechanical such as logging a call in your company's CRM. So, don't fall into the "I don't know" trap. Instead, counter and continue coaching by asking a question such as: *"Okay, you don't know . . . [PAUSE] . . . If you* did *know, what do you think that might sound like?"*

Or you could ask a slightly less tongue-in-cheek question such as "If I weren't here, what would do?" You'll probably break the tension, you might even get a smile or chuckle out of your team member, and they're likely to at least share their opinion.

Remember, coaching is all about empowering your team to make the right decisions for themselves on a continual basis. When you do this, you build confidence. When you build confidence, you earn more respect and trust from your team. When you gain this trust and respect, the team will not only work harder with you when no one is watching, you will also have given them a framework to think through and solve their own problems over the long haul.

Who knows, you may even inspire them to become a leader themselves, which in my opinion is the highest form of leadership you can aspire to attain.

Chapter **9**

Reflections on Sales Leadership

L ooking back on the time I've been managed by others, and the time that I've managed a team, I have so many things I want to share about being a sales manager and leading a team of inside sellers. At times, I felt like I had no control at all. At others, I thought the team was running like a well-oiled machine. It was never perfect, and it was never horrible. Yet most of the learnings came at my highs and lows, not the in-betweens.

As I've already shared, leading an inside sales team is in some ways akin to coaching a team of individual athletes. Specifically, I mean that there's no de facto sense of duty from any individual team member back to the team—at least not the same way it works in a team sport like soccer, football, baseball, and so on. Team-sport members quite literally rely on one another to win games. A quarterback relies on his receivers, a pitcher on the infield/outfield. A direct corollary does not quite exist in the "sport" of sales.

I remember experiencing this clearly when I was a rep. I didn't really pay attention to whether my entire team was at or above 100%. I did, however, care about being on the best team and about my team members all doing well for the most part. So why the disconnect?

Working in an inside sales role where performance improvement plans (PIPs) are always a reality, and your entire

paycheck is often tied purely to your own individual performance, it's difficult not to focus only on one's self. As a result, this
puts a sales manager in a bizarre position. You're expected to
deliver a team-wide number but only through a collection of
individual performances, which you do not directly control. So
how then is a manager supposed to swim against a current that
appears to inherently flow against them? I believe it starts with
the right manager mindset, which for me included the
following:

- First, all managers should avoid viewing themselves as
  managers but instead as personal trainers or coaches.
  The word "manager" implies authority, whereas "coach"
  or "trainer" implies servitude. We don't "manage" people.
  As the saying goes, "You *manage* things, but you *lead*
  people." In my opinion, the manager should bring out
  the very best in an individual and help them meet or
  exceed their potential. At the end of the day, being a sales
  manager is not about you—it's about your people and
  nurturing their success.
- Second, managers should be enablers for their team
  members, and for the division and company they dedicate themselves. They should be an organizing and
  driving force that lubricates the wheels of development,
  progress, and growth for both a company and the
  individuals on the team; not an inhibiting force slowing
  anything down. Again, a leadership role is much more
  about everyone and everything else, and much less
  about you.
- Third, a manager should always be looking around the
  corner for future-oriented scaling opportunities. What
  are we doing that's redundant? What are we doing that's
  inefficient? What are we not sharing with one another, or
  colleagues, that could further benefit our sales force? If
  the leader isn't looking around the bend for what's next

and thinking how to cultivate a successful future, then no one is.

♦ Finally, I believe that sales managers should be stewards for their own future workforce and the development of the company's workforce—at a bare minimum, as it relates to the front line. Building a future pipeline of talent is one of the most important roles a manager can serve.

That said, I realize these are particularly complex topics, the specifics of which should be left to individuals and their leadership teams to determine applicability in the context of their own business and company culture. However, there is one concept here I would like to expand on, and it touches on almost all of those topics I laid out—motivation within an inside sales team. This is probably the single topic that I have also given the most thought to over my first few years as a sales leader. It's also arguably the least tangible, whereas the others I pointed out are tactical, which is why I'm dedicating an entire chapter to this concept.

When I initially started running the team that I ran from 2014 to 2016, I was grasping for a framework to help me help myself. As I thought about it, I remembered a conversation that I had with Tony Williams, the former mayor of Washington, DC. When I was working with him at the Corporate Executive Board (CEB), I remember specifically asking him a question like this:

Tony, in a position of such great power, how did you ever get anything done? Didn't you always have people trying to get your attention so that you could help them push their own agendas ahead?

He responded (and I'm paraphrasing):

Well, it was difficult at first. But when I took the job I knew I would have to stay focused. So, the way I went about it was by

*picking my "three drums"; in other words, the three biggest
things that were the most important to me. I would be relentless
about these three things and if anyone wanted my attention
for something else, I wouldn't spend time on it. Period.*

For those of you who don't know, compared to an array of
other DC mayors, Tony Williams went down as one of the most
well-liked and successful mayors in the city's history.[1] Of
course, I can't say for certain that all his success was attributed
to the three drums, but I'm sure it helped.

So, for lack of a better framework, I figured I would use
Tony's three drums idea to get me on my way. For me, as I've
already touched on in earlier chapters, those were:

1. Coaching
2. Scaling
3. Recruiting

Yet, there was something missing; if these three drums
were the skin, bones, and muscles, then the blood, vital organs,
and nervous system were still missing. That's where understanding motivation came into focus for me.

Now when it comes to the topic of motivation, I certainly
don't claim to be on the level of someone like Daniel Pink—far
from it. But, in my opinion, his research and perspective on
motivation should be required reading not just for sales managers, but for any manager in any function at any business. In
fact, it just so happened that I was using his motivational
framework for well over a year before I even knew it was
something he came up with. Rest assured this wasn't tied to my
own genius; I saw a brief write up on this in a colleague's
Evernote one day, and it resonated so strongly with me that I
couldn't help but adopt it immediately.

Specifically, when he gets into the guts of what motivates
individuals he discusses three very specific things: (1) vision,

(2) autonomy, and (3) the pursuit of mastery. At face value, seasoned sales leaders may think this is nonsense. However, others may realize and appreciate that—specifically when it comes to sales—salespeople are not as motivated by money, or other extrinsic rewards, as they are by intrinsic drivers.

This thinking is backed by a variety of sales consultants and leaders and exemplified well in an article by Next Level Sales Consulting. Here's a quote that jumped at to me (also referenced in a previous chapter):

> *Salespeople who are intrinsically motivated are more fulfilled and financially successful than extrinsically motivated salespeople.*[2]

Still don't believe me? There's some great research from Dave Kurlan and his team at Objective Management Group, highlighted in this article (also referenced in a previous chapter):

> *In the old days (pre-2008), if salespeople were motivated, then they were probably motivated by money. According to data from Objective Management Group, 54% of salespeople were money-motivated during the 1990s and first half of the 2000s. Today, the data shows that no more than 27% of salespeople are what we now call extrinsically-motivated.*[3]

In other words, the compensation and benefits your company offers are simply table stakes. What's worse, they may not even be table stakes! I've hired a variety of team members over the years that have taken less pay to come work at HubSpot because they believe so adamantly in the company's mission and want to help us change the way the world does sales and marketing.

Next is my own analysis of the three ingredients that create motivated individuals and teams, based on Pink's framework.

INGREDIENT #1: VISION

If you are working on something exciting that you really care about, you don't need to be pushed. The vision pulls you.

—Steve Jobs[4]

Do your team members feel like they are part of something truly bigger than themselves? Do they believe that their mission is a noble one, *worthy* of pursuit? Do they believe that what your company does, or the goals you've laid out for your team, are more important and lasting than their own individual accomplishments? The more I've thought about this, the more it makes sense to me. (Almost) everyone wants to be part of something bigger than themselves. They want to make a lasting impact on the world. Just "liking" the products or services their company sells is no longer enough; they must be able to see the larger vision and what role they play in relation to making that vision reality.

Now, in fairness, clearly articulating a vision is an incredibly complicated exercise for a sales manager to successfully complete alone. Reflecting on how I did this, I felt like I only executed one half of the equation well, which was taking our company's mission and vision and translating all the way down to the team and the individual levels. However, the other half of the equation, which I was missing, lay in making a unilateral versus bilateral decision on the team vision itself. If I had the chance to do this over again, I would have started by gathering team feedback through a short survey and then discussing the responses in a small group setting to clarify what they shared in common. I ultimately did go through the second half of this exercise, but it was about a year too late by the time I did. I have laid out the results of each exercise in this book so that you have a framework to build on yourself (see the "artifacts" at the end of this chapter).

INGREDIENT #2: AUTONOMY

Control leads to compliance. Autonomy leads to engagement.
—Daniel Pink[5]

This is a very, very tough one to do well. Many companies still have highly restrictive work policies, most of which make little to no sense to me. Of course, it's also easy for me to say, considering I work for a company that encourages both an unlimited work from home and an unlimited vacation policy, for example.

My take on autonomy is that it's a fancy way to say, "trust and belief that people will do the right thing when no one else is looking." Most individuals want this level of trust, and when it's given to them, they generally respect it. They also often work harder when the decision to work harder, or pull back, comes from within. Of course, the key to making autonomy "work" lies in creating the environment in which the individuals are working is close to, or already operating at, the desired level. This ties back to the idea of consensus, which human beings naturally and instinctively seek—if everyone else is coming in early and leaving late, they don't want to be the only one *not* doing those things. To establish this, I've done a few things that may work for you, too:

- ◆ First, I establish very clear team-wide expectations. When a new team members joins the team, I share our team-wide vision and what it means to work on the team. It's our own kind of warriors' creed.
- ◆ Second, I establish very specific individual-level training expectations. Literally, "here are the things you need to accomplish in month 1, month 2," and so on. In this process, I also clearly define my role, the roles of other team members, the additional support resources that will be made available to them, and in which format.

♦ Finally, I allow my team members to get to work and prove to me that I should continue to give them greater and greater independence, even though I believe this should not be held in a tight fist. If they start falling out of line with either the team-wide expectations I set or the individual expectations I set for them, they will slowly but surely start to lose levels of autonomy. If they ultimately cannot adhere to the team-wide or individual-level expectations, then they are typically engaged in a PIP (performance improvement plan), a 30- to 60-day probationary period in which they must make significant behavioral and performance changes. If those changes are not met we'll likely have a conversation about a new career path.

INGREDIENT #3: PURSUIT OF MASTERY

Education is not the learning of facts, but the training of the mind to think.

—Albert Einstein[6]

A long-term research project commissioned by Middlesex University for Work Based Learning found that from a sample of 4,300 workers, 74% felt that they weren't achieving their full potential at work due to lack of development opportunities.[7]

Moreover, one-third of employees will leave a new job before the first year is over. It shouldn't be this way, and it doesn't have to be this way. Any sales team member, manager, director, or senior leader knows how detrimental losing productive team members earlier than expected—or at all, for that matter—can be. Of course, this doesn't just apply to sales.

I was never quite sure how to articulate the importance of learning and the pursuit of mastery, but I knew it was key to my success as a leader and to my team members' individual success. To achieve this and build it into my team culture, I did several things:

- ♦ First, I verbally expressed it—many times—to bring it to life. "Learning matters. Learning is important. We can all learn something no matter how new, or how experienced we are. It is a worthy end in and of itself." I figured if I just said it aloud and explained the importance of learning to my team that would be a start. It was the power of repetition in action.

- ♦ Second, I made sure to focus on just one "big" skill at a time with every single team member. For new team members, these skills would be simple things like mastering a connect call taking good notes during an exploratory call, or writing properly formatted emails free of typos. For senior team members, skills would include relationship building with team members outside the sales function, tailoring executive-level communication, or negotiating with legal, IT, and procurement teams. Regardless of the tenure or experience level, I always made sure there was one, and only one, skill that I was proactively working on with my team members on a regular basis.

- ♦ Third, I established regular office hours where anything and everything was "in play." It was a safe space. There were no questions too big or too small. In office hours, we covered everything, whether it be from a brand new BDR or a rep with twenty years' experience

- ♦ Fourth, I regularly encouraged (and sometimes forced) team members to work with one another and across teams. I wanted them to understand that no one is successful in sales at HubSpot (or anywhere for that matter, in my opinion) going it alone. There is just no way to develop all the skills necessary in the time available by learning by yourself.

♦ Finally, I'm very fortunate to work for a company that also believes deeply in training and development. For example, every HubSpot employee has $5,000 of credit they can use toward furthering themselves professionally every year. It also has a free book program where any employee can get any book they want paid for by the company.

In a hope to bring much of what I've written about here to life, you'll see a variety of my manager artifacts across the following pages; please also see the Team Vision Document 2014, which appears in Chapter 8. Please feel free to use them however you may see fit for you own teams.

Leadership Artifacts and Examples from My Own Management Experiences

ARTIFACT #1: FIRST ANNUAL RECAP AND 2015 VISION

[NAMES HAVE ALL BEEN CHANGED TO PROTECT THE INNO-CENT/GUILTY. ☺ ANY USE OF A NAME IS PURELY FICTITIOUS.]

Subject Line: 2014 Team Year in Review . . . and How We Win Together in 2015

Team,

I intended to deliver this message far sooner, but seeing as how January hasn't quite passed, I don't think I'm too late. These are my reflections from 2014 and my summary of a collective vision/working plan for 2015.

If I had to pick a theme as we closed 2014 and started a new year it would probably be something to the effect of "Out of the darkness and into the light . . . " Dramatic? Perhaps.

Here's some perspective:

We faced a massive amount of change in 2014. PODS collapsed, Evan and Jemma came back into the funnel with us, we rolled out tons of new tools for Partners, implemented territories, implemented hard lead capacity, implemented hard Partner lead capacity, rolled out tons of product enhancements, were faced with stiffer competition, had to deal with continuously more educated and sophisticated buyers, raised quotas, lost Lacy, lost Abby (then won Abby back:)), lost Emily, lost David, added four new team members, and more . . . *but through all of that, this is what we managed to achieve as a team*:

2014 Team-Wide Highlights

- $A-MM ARR/$B,000 MRR
- Closed/Won X new customers
- Y% annual attainment
- Z% for the 5 months trailing August to December
- #1 team in VAR by ARR
- #2 balance team in VAR
- #2 team in the entire company measured by total ARR ($X-MM was #1)
- #3/4 team in the company (*depending on how you slice the numbers*)
- Had 3 team members in top 10 reps for entire company
- Had 1 of the top 5 VAR BDRs for the year
- Mason #1 Domestic Rep
- Seven promotions across the team
- Eigh out of 11 team members over G% annual attainment
- David and Emily are engaged

(*continued*)

(*continued*)

♦ Evan had a baby . . . and got engaged (just had to one-up David, didn't you?)

On an individual level, I am extremely proud of the commitments you all have made to your own success, our team's success, and HubSpot's success as it rolls on to the 2020 goal of a $Y in revenue.

Now the question we're left to answer is how we're going to get to 140% and the #1 team at HubSpot (both by total MRR and balanced performance), a goal you all shared with me that you wanted to collectively achieve this year.

I can spend time breaking down numbers, doing funnel analysis, showing you exactly how many deals need to close and what the ASP will be. But I don't think that's what's going to motivate any one of you to get there. Instead, what I think motivates that performance is how we work together.

Here's my promise to you as we work together to attain 140% and claim the sole seat at the top of HubSpot in 2015.

I will focus on leading across three major areas at all times:

♦ Coaching—I will ask myself (and act on) every day what I am personally doing to help each and every one of you get to both your personal and professional goals.

♦ Scaling—I will ask myself (and act on) every day what I am personally doing to find points of leverage that will make our entire team's sales operations smoother and faster.

♦ Recruiting—I will ask myself (and act on) every day what I'm doing to get "the right people on the right bus at the right time," ensuring that as we change and build the team, our talent density gets higher and higher.

All three of these working "guideposts" were designed with intent. They were designed with you in mind, with our team in mind, and with HubSpot's long-term vision in mind. And while I know that money motivates all of you, the way I want to inspire you to achieve your personal and professional goals goes beyond money. My belief is that my motivational philosophy needs to tap into your core.

As I shared with you all a few weeks ago, here's how I think about motivation, drive and resilience . . . and if I'm ever breaking these principles, you need to tell me. Please hold me accountable, or else the wheels will begin to fall off our bus.

Throughout all my work with you, and with each other, in 2015 I will:

Inspire a sense of higher purpose—I mean this in so far as showing you clearly that what you each do, what our team does, and what HubSpot does truly matters and makes a difference in other people's lives.

Lead you in the pursuit of mastery—you'll know that at long as you're on this team and at HubSpot, you are building skills here that you will carry with you throughout your career, and that ideally will last a lifetime.

Instill a deep sense of autonomy—I want you all to be masters of your own universe. The truth is that you all have personal goals and motivations for coming into work every day and grinding through the sales funnel. To achieve those personal goals, you also have professional goals. Running your own book of business and crushing your sales numbers is, in part, what allows you to accomplish those personal endeavors. My intent here

(continued)

(*continued*)

is to help you accelerate toward independence, even though I will always be ready to help every step of the way. I will always do my best to demonstrate trust and defer to your judgment, so long as you continuously practice our company's mantra, "Use good judgment."

Now, finally, this is my "ask" from each of you as we collectively work together toward the common goal of becoming the #1 team at the company (many of you may recognize these from a certain HubSpot Veteran at the VAR helm):

- *You must have a desire to be successful in sales,*
- *You must be committed to do whatever it takes to be successful,*
- *You must have the ability to take responsibilities for sales outcomes, and*
- *You must maintain a positive outlook on the products and services we sell, the company we work for, and yourself.*

That's it. Those are my only "asks" of you as we work together and climb the $Y mountain. Combined with my "gives," I believe we'll be able to achieve all of our goals together and then some.

Now let's dig in, band together, and focus on the task at hand. I know we can all do this.

Here's to a hugely successful 2015 for HubSpot, the VAR Team, to our team collectively, and to each and every one of you individually.

Onward and upward,

Sig

ARTIFACT 2: FIRST MAJOR TEAM SUCCESS

[NAMES HAVE ALL BEEN CHANGED TO PROTECT THE INNO-CENT/GUILTY. ☺ ANY USE OF A NAME IS PURELY FICTITIOUS.]

Subject Line: April Reflections—Why X% Was the Result and *Not* the True Goal

Team,

   I've been doing some reading and thinking this morning and wanted to share some reflections from April, our year-to-date, and my three years at HubSpot.

   First, I want to congratulate you all again on a truly outstanding performance in April. We collectively smoked our numbers and claimed the #1 team spot in the company. There were some monster performances, including:

   Braden—300% of his goal and, I believe, taking back the record for most MRR sold in a month by a domestic VAR rep

   Rebecca—125%, which seals her 12-month "trend" (not going to call it out by name), and 99% sure sealing her promotion to Sr. IMS

   Cal—105%, which is the third month in a row he's been up and over the 100% watermark; really great progress

   Mark—150%, closing four deals on his own, and transitioning into his new IMS role

   Jillian—97%, making some last-minute saves on a big deal by teaming closely with our Services Team and setting her partners up for long-term success, as always

   Jemma—204%, going out with a bang and who will be missed by us all for a myriad of reasons

(continued)

(continued)

Evan—113%, who has only missed once in literally as long as I can remember and has T12M performance of 140%

Gary—108%, which by his measuring stick may be considered a light month, but was a truly impressive feat coming off a $Z+ March

Matt—Just under 100%, and putting up his second best month in the funnel since he started measured by MRR

Sam—Never saying "die," showing grit, doing all he could to close as much as possible, AND taking down his first two channel deals like a pro

Ken—Going above and beyond in preparing for his transition to IMS; he's dedicated an enormous amount of time to mastering the IMA and beginning to learn the platform from top to bottom

As I looked back and asked myself, "Why?" or "How did we do it?" or "What makes this team different?" I could have concluded many things. Hard work, pipeline building, incredible control of the sales process, endless hours invested, a deep understanding of the product, unmatched value in our Partner Program, the ability of our Partners to overperform month in and month out, our marketing team, our sales enablement team, or any combination of those things. But the longer I thought about it, the more convinced I became that there was an underpinning reason. A reason that trumped all the others. A reason that led to all of the "other things" happening. That reason? Put simply, selling with noble purpose. It was for this reason that X% team-level attainment was the result and not the true goal. Rather, the true goal was selling with a noble purpose itself.

You may remember that earlier in the year I sent out a really long email, similar to this one, where in part I articulated my leadership style. There were (at least) three things I wanted you to hold me accountable to, which were:

1. Inspiring a sense of higher purpose
2. Leading you in the pursuit of mastery
3. Instilling a deep sense of autonomy

Quite frankly, I've always known what #1 meant, but have struggled to articulate it beyond the chatter in my mind. I think I have it down now, so here's my take on what our higher purpose is—our noble purpose—as HubSpot Team Members, Sales/VAR Team Members, and "Team Sig" Team Members:

At a company level . . .

We are not just selling a sales and marketing software platform. We are changing the way the world does sales and marketing. The same way that Google transformed the way the world finds and accesses information we, too, are enabling a fundamental change in the lives of sales and marketing professionals all over the world.

At a software level . . .

We are not selling a software, or even a methodology, that allows businesses to generate more traffic, leads, and sales. Instead, we are helping businesses amplify their voice and build their brand. We are making people's lives—yes, real people's lives—that work in both sales and marketing, easier, less stressful, and more efficient every day. We are helping marketers foster better relationships with the people that interact with their brand. Alongside that, we're making it possible for salespeople to have truly relevant conversations with people that may actually need their business's help. And from a business owner's perspective,

(continued)

(*continued*)

we are making the growth of their company both more predictable and profitable. We are arming them with the information and tools they need to make smarter decisions about how to spend money, how to hire, when to hire, and how to add continuous value to their base of customers and prospects. We are eradicating irrelevant conversations from happening. We are eliminating waste in the system. We are fundamentally making people's lives better, global commerce better, and creating a better world in the process.

At the Partner Program level . . .

We are not simply helping agencies shift from projects to retainers. We are not simply helping them expand and learn new services. We are not simply helping them demonstrate better ROI. And we are not simply helping them learn a new sales process. Instead, we are transforming their ability to see into and plan for the future. We are educating them on how to add even more value to their customers in new and unexpected ways. We are making the delivery of their professional services to clients efficient, logical, and meaningful. We are helping them make a truly meaningful impact on their clients' businesses. We are helping them make a profound difference in the trajectory of their business, their own lives, and the lives of the people they employ. We are making a dent in their universe, and that dent is growing every single day.

And at a team level . . .

We are not simply focused on using the people we talk to every day as a means to an end. We are not simply aiming at hitting X% month in and month out. We are not simply striving to be the A sales team at HubSpot. We are part of something bigger. Something that started before you. Something that started before "Team Sig." Something that started before "Team H." And something that started before VAR or HubSpot ever existed. We are the ground level force that drives change in the world. The force that makes it possible for people to have better interactions. The force that drives a better way to consume information. The force that enables better decision making. And a force that is making a difference in far more people's lives than you will likely ever be able to actually see.

So as you look ahead to May, to the rest of the year, the next phone call you make, or next email you respond to, ask yourself this: *"How will this customer—and how will this person—be different as a result of doing business with us?"*

Focusing on that single question, perhaps alongside the notes in this message, is what will enable us all to continually sell with a noble purpose. This is our goal. Everything that follows is simply the result.

Congratulations again on a great April and very strong start to the year. I'm looking forward to participating in and seeing the big things we'll go on to accomplish in 2015 together.

Onward and upward,

Sig

ARTIFACT 3: FIRST MAJOR TEAM FAILURE

*[NAMES HAVE ALL BEEN CHANGED TO PROTECT THE INNO-
CENT/GUILTY. ☺ ANY USE OF A NAME IS PURELY FICTITIOUS.]*

Subject Line: June 2015—Team Sig—Why Our Team
Missed and What We're Doing about It

H, P, and T,

I have no excuses to share with you. Our team missed our
[Month] 2015 number and, quite frankly, I am very disappointed and embarrassed by it. Delivering this number to
the business is my responsibility, and my responsibility
alone. Everyone on the team worked their tails off, but it
is my fault that we did not deliver. In the three years that I've
been in the funnel as a manager or as a rep, this team (under
D's leadership and mine) has only missed twice. This
performance was unacceptable by my standards, my team's
standards, and HubSpot's standards. We are far better than
this.

We finished the month at $X on a goal of $Y, or 95%. In
addition, we sold just under $Z in 2nd URLs and Double
Comp so I'm considering our finish closer to Y% than X%.
While we had A out of B reps hit over 100%, we still fell
short.

Here are my thoughts on why this happened:

1. Early Rep Attrition

    Jemma and Cal both left the funnel earlier than I
    had anticipated. We had planned for Jemma to
    leave for some time; Cal, however, was completely
    unexpected. With both of them out, that left about a
    $X gap in our number, not accounting for padding

we were granted at the beginning of the year. I could have planned better for this.

2. Subpar New Hire Onboarding

I learned some lessons the hard way in my first 10 months managing. We brought on 3 new hires in my first 5 months, then promoted 2 BDRs, and hired 2 new BDRs in the next 5 months. At one point our team was up to 12 team members. I thought I could pair the new hires—Mark, Sam, and Cal—with peer mentors, join/run calls for 3 to 5 sales cycles each, run group training 3x/week and let them run from there. I was wrong. I underestimated the amount of energy, attention, effort, and time they would need to get ramped up. As a result, Cal left, Mark went on a 90 day plan (which he just came off today), and Sam is now going on a 30 day plan starting today. Their long-term production deficit caught up with us in both [Month] and [Month]. I take full responsibility for not providing them with everything necessary to succeed.

3. New Hires Could Not Close Gap

To backfill for Jemma and Cal, we promoted Mark and Ken to IMS. They were both Associate IMS when they were promoted, had been IMA certified, software certified, and had run between 4 and 5 sales processes end to end with little to no help before their official promotions. However, as we all know, being an IMS is far different than being a BDR. With a combined quota of $X this —which they met collectively—this was still not enough to close the gap we faced—$Y (rep rollup vs. team quota). I did not put the right plan in place to ensure their success.

(continued)

(*continued*)

4. Insufficient Time Dedicated to Recruiting

While I feel like I've dedicated a lot of time to sourcing candidates—about Z in the past 6 months—this has also proven to be an area for improvement. If I had more "go to" candidates in my funnel and didn't have to rely on promoting my two BDRs to the IMS role, I suspect we could have been more productive. I have changed my behavior on this and have outlined my plan below.

5. Slight ASP Dropoff

The data here are inconclusive, but thought I'd share the numbers with you. For the first half of the year, this is what our deal flow and ASP looked like:

January—$A; H deals
February—$B; I deals
March—$C; J deals
April—$D; K deals
May—$E; L deals
June—$F; M deals

As you can see, we started to experience a slight uptrend in March ($A), April ($B), and May ($C). We subsequently experienced a drop-off in June down to $W ASP. Even if we pull from the low end and say that the target should be right around $A, that $B per deal gap multiplied through X deals would've generated an additional $C MRR. If we hit the high end of the range at $D, we would have generated an additional $E MRR—either of which would have closed our gap. I'm still not sure if there's something systemic happening or if it's an anomaly. I'm going to keep my eye on this closely in the coming months.

You may also be wondering about pipeline generated. We've kept this steady at or above X opps/month. This is the goal we set at the beginning of the year and we've kept up this pace. At an average close rate of A% opp created to close that yields about B deals/month which we've been in the ballpark of all year and has produced the right results for the most part (average sales cycle ~Z days).

If there are other things you think I should be paying attention to, or that you think may have contributed to this underperformance, I'm open to hearing your feedback.

With that said, this is what we're doing to fix it and get back to the A–Z% trajectory we've tracked at for almost a year:

Please keep in mind that all the plans outlined here are designed to "tune up the engine," not tear it down and rebuild it from scratch. I'm also trying to focus my energy solely on controllable factors.

1. Build My Recruiting Muscle

    The fact that I did not have a sufficient pipeline of reps teed up to join my team is not acceptable. I dedicated time here and there—from no time at all in a week to more than a day in a week. This inconsistency did not drive the volume of conversations I needed to have and as a result we suffered collectively. My plan is to block 2 hours twice per week (4 hours) on nothing but recruiting and to treat that time like they're all closing calls. In addition, I'm going to build "referral development" into my 1:1s with team members every week.

(continued)

(*continued*)

2. Double Down on Reps and BDRs with Less Than One Year in the Funnel

For the past month, I've been doing "double sessions" with Mike and Sam. This approach has kept them motivated and produced higher levels of accountability than I've seen in the past. It also helped me uncover areas of true weakness. This worked well for Mike, but did not produce the necessary results for Sam. I'm going to continue this intensive daily coaching with the two of them. As for Cal and Mark, I've instituted a "mandatory deal buddy" policy. They are required to bring at least one other team member (myself included) into their deals for as many stages possible and to split all deals they close until they get to between A and B closed won opps. If we were on the direct side, I would see this as risky. However, the senior members of my team are farming and have mostly gotten their partners to a point where they are fairly productive on their own. Therefore, it's my belief that they have the extra bandwidth to help these newer team members—many also have management aspirations so this should prove to be a fair training environment for them. Finally, for the BDRs, my sole focus is on "wind sprints" every week—in other words, focusing purely on training, role-play, and call reviews. My thought process here is that if they have their talk tracks down early and keep their activity high, the results will follow.

3. Learn from the Team

This includes learning both from my team members as well as from my manager peers. For example, I'm soliciting feedback from the team both on a group basis and on a one-on-one basis. On the group level, I've asked the team to fill out a "start/stop/keep" survey today. My goal here is to learn about things the team thinks are working and those that aren't. Survey responses are anonymous to drive maximum candor. I also haven't figured out quite yet how I'm going to leverage/work with my manager peers, but I know I need to learn from those that have traveled the road before me. I'm going to keep working on that.

4. Continue Building for Scale

Finally, as I've tried to do both during my time as a rep and manager, I will continue to build for scale at the company level, testing first at the team level. For example, I feel strongly that our team is not as well versed as it should be in selling against competitors nor is it as well trained as it should be in our product from end to end (i.e., Enterprise Product). To correct that, I'm leaning on some team members as well as the sales enablement and sales engineering teams to run regular team training sessions across the months of [Month 1] and [Month 2]. As I identify additional "one to many" areas of opportunity—that will allow my team members, VAR, the Sales Org, and HubSpot—to work smarter, not harder, I'll focus my attention on those opportunities as they come.

Again, if there are areas you think I'm missing, your feedback would be appreciated. I'm committed to turning this around and crushing our numbers through the end of 2015. Our plan requires us to deliver $X-MM to the

(*continued*)

(continued)

business this year and we've already delivered \$Y-MM in the first half. I'm confident we can deliver over \$Z-MM by the end of the year with continued focus, will, and execution.

Onward and upward,

Sig

ARTIFACT 4: TEAM-DRIVEN VISION DOC

[NAMES HAVE ALL BEEN CHANGED TO PROTECT THE INNOCENT/GUILTY. ☺ ANY USE OF A NAME IS PURELY FICTITIOUS.]

TEAM SIG—2015/2016—IDENTITY, NONNEGOTIABLES, AND COMMON ASPIRATIONS

1. VALUES AND NONNEGOTIABLES

Sense of Higher Purpose—Contributing to something bigger than—from team members to partners to the division to the company

Autonomy—The freedom to do what you want when you want without restriction or hesitation so long as it does not trample on the freedoms of another.

Accountability—Ownership for all actions we take and decisions we make, regardless of the outcome; a culture of responsibility, not blame.

Dependability—Each of us is willing to help for the greater good. Whether it be coverage while people are out, mentoring, coaching, shadowing—help is available.

(continued)

(*continued*)

Honesty, Transparency, and Respect—Honesty and Transparency: HubSpot is built on it, and we think that it is impossible to build any sort of relationship without honesty. Respect: For one another both personally and in a work setting. We think being respected is more important than being liked.

Professional Excellence—Always striving to improve; knowing we do not know everything

Competition—Seen as a valuable end in itself and used as a motivating force

2. PASSIONS

Continuous Learning/Pursuit of Mastery—We are always striving for better ways to do things (smarter not harder) and getting to the goal. We strive to learn more to aspire to be leaders and take charge. Each one of us is the master of our own destiny.

Teamwork—We all help each other, and Partners, in many ways. We help each other grow, dream, and work more efficiently. Everyone is friendly and outgoing, quirky in their own way. Sharing our ideas helps us with different viewpoints that form a cohesive, amazing team. Each of us is willing to help for the greater good. Whether it be coverage while people are out, mentoring, coaching, shadowing—help is available.

Work/Life Balance—Achieve your goals and do it in a smart way. If you can get it done in a different way than others but it works for you, that's fine as long as you achieve the goals set out.

(*continued*)

(continued)

FOOD/TRAVEL/TEAM OUTINGS

3. ASPIRATIONS

Company-Wide Top Performance—PCLUB attainment for everyone on the team, every year—making 100% is not enough or acceptable.

Respect and Pride—Be proud of what we build, have built, and help our Partners build; to be respected and trusted by our peers and Partners.

Professional Development and Advancement—Promotions, Mastering Sales, Mastering Leadership, Mentoring one another.

Be a team of leaders—We all take complete ownership of the work and outcomes we achieve, for better or worse.

Financial Independence—Support family, provide for myself, live comfortably.

4. TEAM NAME OR MANTRA

Onward and Upward

Part 4

What Inbound Selling Means across the Executive Suite

Chapter **10**

Sales Is a Team Sport
The Executives' Guide to Transforming into an Inbound Sales Organization

The pages in this chapter contain a series of four interviews I ran across late 2015 and early 2016 with a variety of cross-functional leaders from HubSpot. Despite the fact the premise of this book is that too little is shared from a front-line rep perspective, that does not mean I don't value the perspective of highly experienced business leaders. In addition, for any inbound sales, inside sales, or outside sales organization to be successful, it requires near-perfect synchronization across a variety of functional areas. For those reasons, I decided it was important to gain those deep, cross-functional executive perspectives and share them here with you. The interview series, which was edited for accuracy and length, is laid out as follows:

- Part 1—Inbound Selling and the Future of the Sales Function: An Interview with Hunter Madeley, Chief Sales Officer, HubSpot, Inc.
- Part 2—How to Create Sales and Marketing Alignment to Drive Growth: An Interview with Kipp Bodnar, Chief Marketing Officer, HubSpot, Inc.

- Part 3—The Role of Sales Enablement to Fuel Revenue Growth: An Interview with Debbie Farese, Head of Sales Enablement (2013–2016), HubSpot, Inc.
- Part 4—Building a Sales Operations Team to Set Up Growth: An Interview with David McNeil, VP Global Sales Operations (2014–2016), HubSpot, Inc.

Part 1: Inbound Selling and the Future of the Sales Function

AN INTERVIEW WITH HUNTER MADELEY, CHIEF SALES OFFICER, HUBSPOT[1]
December 2015. Edited for length and clarity.

BRIAN: Hunter, today I'd love to chat about how you lead a sales team that is taking more of a modern sales approach. But let's start with how you began your career in sales.

HUNTER: I got pulled in through my network—I think my friends knew I would enjoy the profession of sales before I did. Through university I was always okay not knowing exactly the path I was going to take—I had faith that success would follow my interests. I was interested in business. I was interested in team dynamics. I was always part of teams, whether that be sports, academics, or otherwise and the goals of the team always felt bigger than my personal success. I was drawn to the idea that you could be part of something bigger, that you could play a role in contributing to a broad goal.

I was doing a bunch of cool stuff in sports and event marketing very early in my career. Then a good friend of mine cornered me, saying, "Here's why the world of sales is so interesting. You happen to make a bunch of money if you're good at it, and being good at it means helping others solve problems." I believed him, went and had a few interviews and met a bunch of great people. I realized that there are common threads of both competitive and collaborative DNA in people that love sales and that seemed to align really well with my view of the world. I just loved the people and teams I was meeting with so I jumped in and took on quota. I've been responsible for revenue ever since.

BRIAN: Did the vision your friend painted match reality?

HUNTER: Yeah, for the most part. The vision painted was clear because I was dealing with a rep who had been selling for a couple years. I'd say the vision that was painted for me by the hiring managers was fairly clear too. It wasn't too dissimilar from what I actually experienced. The day to day is tough to accurately describe until you get into the grind of a quota-carrying role. It's exhausting and exhilarating at once. Then you need to decide whether or not it's a life for you. It takes a certain type of person to have a number over their head, that you didn't choose, but are expected to operate against every day, every week, and every month. You either love it or you don't. I love it.

BRIAN: What was selling like back then?

HUNTER: I started B2B selling in earnest in 1995, and before that was in "light sales" role selling sponsorship to events managed by our company. Day to day, it was not too dissimilar from the world we're in now. I have a little bit of an oppositional view to the assumption that the world of professional sales has fundamentally changed. The ways in which we engage have changed as technology has enabled buyers and sellers to create new value exchange platforms, but the purpose has remained the same. The goal of all companies, most often pursued by those folks in go-to-market functions, is to build credibility and trust with prospects and to create value for customers. Then your happy customers become an extension of your go-to-market team. The ways in which we build trust and credibility through the sales process have evolved, but in general, the job is very similar now to what is was back then.

And great companies have always created "inbound" interest—word-of-mouth is inbound in its most elemental form. I remember an old shampoo commercial from the late seventies which explicitly called out the power of building a social network around your brand. The commercial ended with the spokeswoman saying, "It's so good, you'll tell two friends, and they'll tell two friends, and so on, and so on . . ." With every "and so on," the number of faces in the shot doubled. By the final frame of the commercial the screen was filled with people. That's the idea: Do good work. Offer great value. Build trust and credibility. Let your customers be an extension of your sales team. That's how we've always grown successful businesses.

If we look at the interesting world of B2B sales decades past, we saw buyers who operated differently than the general consumer. We were typically selling more complex and expensive products and services to those buyers, and there were much fewer of them than in a B2C environment. So, the opportunity to leverage mass communication was limited. Instead, we had to figure how to build targeted communication plans and create opportunities to engage like trade shows and special events. But it was all fulfilling the same purpose—to build trust and credibility and to pull the right buyers into an evaluation. Each event, conversation, mailing, or phone call was providing energy into the system, and we were trying to get an inbound word-of-mouth flywheel going. The way in which we started that flywheel has always depended on the technology available at the time and the really cool thing is we have great tech that's getting better every day. We can be significantly smarter, more efficient, more helpful, and connect more personally than ever before. It's a great time to be a growth professional.

BRIAN: You take a more targeted approach to sales now, yes?

HUNTER: The question is how do you build a genuine, personal, contextual relationship. Go-to-market engines work hard to connect the strategic, operational, financial, and personal goals of the prospect to the solutions they provide. And they lay out a future state that is compelling enough to begin a change management initiative. People generally avoid change, so you need to build a bunch of momentum. Technology moves fast and provides all sorts of new ways to engage and build momentum in more targeted ways. But we humans evolve slowly; we make decisions about the relationships that matter to us and engage with each other on similar terms that we've used for centuries. Technology enables new ways to connect, but the decision to invest more time and energy into a relationship with a person or brand is made using age-old frameworks. Buyers need to trust the people and the brand before they'll commit to a change.

BRIAN: Right. It sounds like the underlying need hasn't changed in your opinion then, right? What role did technology play in the late 1990s, when you were coming up in your sales career? How different is it today, if at all?

HUNTER: Basic CRM became really important in the mid to late nineties. You could use it to organize and plan without developing your own system in house. It leveled the playing field a bit and gave sales professionals more time to focus on building relationships. Today, we're seeing that sales professionals are typically needed at a much later stage in the buying cycle, and they aren't needed for a bunch of products that were once the domain of a quota-carrying rep. Clearly, there aren't door-to-door vacuum sales reps or door-to-door vinyl siding salespeople anymore. A bunch of products and industries have been commoditized and have a bunch of new distribution channels, the most dominant being Amazon. But other industries and products have taken their place. The sales profession is really well aligned to a business when the buyer is making a team-based, considered purchase that demands a change in process, systems, and possibly talent. And it's also really well aligned when the buyer needs help in assessing the current issues and missed opportunities.

BRIAN: I think that there may always be a need for a salesperson of some type, but part of what I'm thinking is that perhaps the volume and way in which a sales professional operates may be significantly different in the future. For example, the Corporate Executive Board famously states that over 60 percent of the buying decision-making process is done before a buyer ever gets on the phone with, or meets, the sales rep.

HUNTER: Yep. That's data that's cited pretty often. The buyer is much more educated by the time they engage with a sales rep. That puts a bunch of responsibility on the rep to really know her stuff. Since the nineties we've been talking about the demise of the sales rep, but I believe it was Daniel Pink who called out the census data that shows the number of sales professionals has been increasing over time. There aren't many folks running around selling access to the Yellow Pages today, but there are tens of thousands of folks selling ad space on the biggest social networks. Where you have a market with competing and complex products, you'll have sales teams.

BRIAN: Would you attribute that to the fact that inside selling is now far more prevalent than it was before?

HUNTER: Yeah. There have always been products that *could* be sold inside, but the buyers demanded face-to-face contact. Now the buyers are very comfortable, and often prefer, to leverage technology to manage the full evaluation. What's being created is a new value exchange platform where both sides are interested in building those relationships without needing to rely on face-to-face meetings. That just didn't happen 10 years ago.

The strength and the value of an inside sales team, if it's done well, is that you can sit a bunch of people together, get them to learn from one another and leverage them for real-time feedback about how the market is responding to your products and services. You can adjust behavior and messaging pretty quickly, compared to when you had distributed field teams spread across a bunch of markets. Imagine years ago, when something material changed in the market conditions for that field sales team, it would be really difficult to aggregate that feedback real time and adjust—now, with great inside sales teams, that can happen in minutes.

And so, you could say that the new inside sales paradigm creates a really interesting competitive advantage for a business. But there have always been interesting new ways to run go-to-market engines. And as we figure out new ways to leverage technology and process to drive success, everyone else is simultaneously absorbing that, including our competitors, so the lasting competitive advantage is not the tech or paradigm, it's the execution and the focus on building trust and credibility with every interaction.

An extension of that is to say the sales profession is even more important now than it has ever been. Years ago, the products we built and sold had a certain shelf life of differentiation built into them. It was difficult to be a fast follower. If you built a great product, you had some runway to create sustainable differentiation.

There is almost no sustainable differentiation in products today, especially in software. It's easy to duplicate. Easy to be a fast follower. Your sustainable differentiated value is your go-to-market engine— how quickly and effectively you build trust and deliver value is your differentiation. Doing it at a world-class level is really hard and therefore really hard to copy. It's your brand promise. It's your people. It's the relationships they build. It's the value you provide throughout the customer journey that provides sustainable differentiation. Given that, I think the sales profession is more valuable today than it has ever been.

Part 2: How to Create Sales and Marketing Alignment to Drive Growth

An Interview with Kipp Bodnar, Chief Marketing Officer, HubSpot[2]
December 2015. Edited for length and clarity.

Brian: Kipp, thanks for chatting with me. Why don't we start off by you explaining a little bit about how you came to HubSpot, and how you ultimately rose to the top of the marketing team here.

Kipp: It started with a blog of mine about a decade ago about marketing, and mostly social channels. I was living in North Carolina; it was a fun, fun time. I had worked in a bunch of different marketing agencies at the time, so I was on the agency side of the world and getting so much exposure to a wide variety of marketing tactics.

Brian: Were you working full-time at these agencies?

Kipp: Yeah, I was working full-time and basically worked a standard workweek at the agency. My wife was a teacher at the time, so she had to go to school pretty early. Basically, I would blog from 6:15 a.m. to about 8:30 a.m. and then I'd run upstairs, shower, and get to work by nine o'clock. I lived close to my job. I'd do that, and then I'd come back home and do the same thing in the evening. I did that for a couple of years.

The blog was doing pretty well, getting some traffic, and I started speaking at some conferences and met Rick Burns, who was on the marketing team at HubSpot at the time. He eventually said, "Hey, you should come talk to some of my colleagues working at HubSpot."

Eventually, I talked to Mike Volpe and Brian Halligan and Dharmesh Shah, and I thought those guys were great. My wife, Tera, and I talked about it, and we decided to make the move to Boston. We sold our house, sold our cars, and moved. I basically spent 24 hours of my life in Boston before deciding to move here and work at HubSpot, a company of less than 100 people at the time.

BRIAN: When did you join HubSpot?

KIPP: The start of 2010, when we were still in the Cambridge Innovation Center. My first job was running the HubSpot blog.

BRIAN: Okay, so your first job was running the HubSpot blog. How did it grow from its infancy to what it is today?

KIPP: Dharmesh (HubSpot's co-founder and CTO) was HubSpot's first blogger. Most people forget that. Dharmesh and then Mike (Volpe) and then a bunch of people were doing it part time. My job was focused on figuring out how to start scaling it. When I started, it was still at about 150,000 visits a month (*as of 2017, HubSpot Blogs generate more than 4 million visits per month*). It had already really blown up by then, just from Dharmesh, Mike, and others writing really good articles.

There also just wasn't a lot of competition in the marketplace at the time, and so the content we were writing really stuck out. Then I scaled the work from there, and I think by the time I was a year or two into it we were up to 500,000 to 700,000 visits. We had grown it substantially, and it's obviously continued to scale as we've grown the company over the last six years.

BRIAN: I think anyone hearing this story might say, "Hey, Kipp that's great, but are there a few things that you feel like you did really well? Was this a technology thing? Was it all about hiring people? Were you just lucky?"

Kipp: We hosted everything on HubSpot so we did use technology. So the technology did its thing, and we were only a few people but we could create a lot of content. Part of being successful is grinding it out and you grind it out through being really focused on what you're trying to accomplish.

I think we were always clear on what the goals were, and we were always good at backing out of those goals and understanding what type of activity was going to lead to success around those goals specifically. We were also really good at getting other people on a marketing team, on the services team, and across the company to contribute content and to contribute to the work that we were doing on the blog. We'd take their awesome ideas and package them and optimize them in a way to get the most social spread and email distribution to our subscriber base. That was the difference that allowed us to really scale the sheer volume of people who were seeing our content faster than ever.

Brian: I was a direct beneficiary of all this hard work, so thank you. I just want to change gears a little bit and talk about the idea behind sales and marketing alignment. In your opinion, what is the current state of sales and marketing alignment? What are you seeing?

Kipp: I think the state of the world is that it has progressed, but still has a way to go. If you talk to the most progressive marketing and sales leaders, they have really good marketing-sales alignment with each other, but there's still a large part of the industry that's building that out.

Quite frankly, part of this is a technology issue. Marketing software is relatively new and can still be difficult to connect with sales software. It's a circular system, so until you have that data flowing between the two teams, with each team able to act and get feedback from the other, it's hard to have alignment on anything.

The benefit we have at HubSpot is that we've got great tools in place to have good alignment from the start, and as a result, the data needed to be successful. I think people now are doing a much better job saying that the marketing team's job is to be accountable for results and demand for a sales team, which is in addition to its historical responsibilities, such as driving the brand, the communications, the website presence, and a lot of other things.

I think sales has also done a great job of responding and saying *"Hey, there's a different way to sell here."* We don't have to cold call and just crush ourselves in order to get in front of the right people.

If we take the right approach on the marketing side and combine it with the right messaging on the sales side it can be really effective. I think, if we look at HubSpot customers themselves as an example, the ones that are doing it are doing it well and it works.

BRIAN: If a business owner, marketing leader, or sales leader wanted to start taking those first steps to get to sales and marketing alignment, would you recommend that they actually make it someone's sole responsibility, or not?

KIPP: Yeah, the marketing and sales leaders are the people ultimately responsible. We work to delegate, right? You mentioned operations, too. One of the very first things to do is get an operations person to make sure that the data between the two teams—across whatever systems you're using—works, and you have access to that data. By virtue of that integration, everybody can be held accountable. That's an operations function, and it's an important one.

I think what's interesting on the flipside of that, though, is marketing takes a slightly higher leadership role, not simply because it's marketing; but because marketing's function is to actually *be* first. If your business is going to go into a new market, you're going to first start marketing to that market so your people know your business is there before a sales rep tries connecting with anyone at all. Marketing is the first mover when it comes to growing the business.

BRIAN: I want to fast-forward to the end of what success looks like and then take a quick step back into the middle so we can see how to get there. Let's fast-forward to the end. How does someone know when sales and marketing alignment is working?

KIPP: It's working when the company's successful in meeting its objectives, which is usually tied to a revenue number. You also know it's working when good feedback loops exist between both the sales and marketing teams. Sales knows how many leads they're getting, they know the quality of those leads, they know those leads are properly scored or prioritized, and those leads are made accessible to them in a timely fashion. Marketing knows it's successful when they know that sales is following up on the leads being generated in a timely manner, and that those leads are converting into quality sales opportunities, customers, or both.

Those are some types of metrics you would look at. And success is realized when those metrics are fully understood, agreed upon, and instantaneously accessible by both the sales and marketing parts of the equation. When we look at our metrics at HubSpot, that's really it. If we can share that information with each other, we can be in good alignment. We do, and we are.

BRIAN: Going back to the middle of this process, you also mentioned that when you're trying to stand up some form of sales and marketing alignment you need someone in operations to make sure your marketing systems and sales systems are working together. Could you elaborate a little bit more on the topics of technology, people, and process?

KIPP: I think your pillars are fair ones. On the technology side, you need to ask yourself if you're collecting the right information and tracking the right information. Collected over time, it needs to give you the historical insight to understand how to optimize and improve things in the future. At most companies, there's traditionally some type of marketing software system like HubSpot or another marketing automation system as well as some type of CRM system. Then there's just a bunch of other stand-alone sales and marketing tools, and you can hold onto those as well. You kind of have that infrastructure on the technology side.

On the people side, you need people selling, and people doing the actual marketing campaign work. Then you need some ops people who are making sure the systems are talking to each other. You'd be surprised how much stuff changes. For example, are you asking the right questions so that you get the right information about your leads in order for your sales reps to properly identify and connect with them? You're not going to get that correct right off the bat. You're going to go through separate iterations of that, so having an operations person who can help lead the charge on something like that is going to be really important.

On the process side of things, you want to automate as much as possible, and you want to be as transparent as possible. For example, there need to be crystal clear expectations and visibility into what the marketing team and sales team are committing to one another. Here at HubSpot, we build and share dashboards that anybody can see, publically available to anyone in the company at all times.

BRIAN: What other words of wisdom might you share with people reading this?

KIPP: It's about setting very clear expectations and getting everybody to agree to those expectations.

Beyond sales and marketing alignment, whether you're a tactical marketer, a seller, a sales manager, or a marketing manager, it really comes down to focus. Are you prioritizing the right things? Are you clear on what you're focused on and equally clear on what you're *not* focused on?

BRIAN: Anything else you'd like to share, Kipp?

KIPP: Sure. I think you're fooling yourself if you think any of this is easy. It's not easy, but it's also not rocket science. My advice to the marketers of the world is to not overcomplicate things. Most marketers get obsessed with tools and features and database segmentation to the nth degree in a way that is no longer productive.

Be crystal clear on what you're trying to accomplish.
Keep the solution to a strategy as simple as possible.
You can be really successful if you're doing those
things and you're solving problems.

Last, the thing we really didn't talk about today was
solving for the prospect or the customer. But really
optimizing all of your work across a company for
what that person—the customer—wants, and what
that person needs, is the central thesis of inbound in
general. If you're really solving for those people, and
you're focused in the way that you're solving for
them, you're going to be hugely successful. If, on
the other hand, you're focused on how to create a
new list through your software and sending a person
a tenth email this month, then you're completely
missing the point.

Part 3: The Role of Sales Enablement to Fuel Revenue Growth

An Interview with Debbie Farese, Head of Sales Enablement
(2013–2016), HubSpot[3]
December 2015. Edited for length and clarity.

Brian: Debbie, I have been a very direct beneficiary of all the
great work that you and your team have done over
the years. The point of our chat today is to shed some
light on what the sales enablement function is, how it
operates, how it interfaces with operations teams,
marketing teams, sales teams, et cetera. I just want
to start off by thanking you and I would love to
hear just a little of your story of how you came to
HubSpot.

DEBBIE: I started my career in finance and then transitioned to marketing in the tech space after getting my MBA at MIT Sloan. I spent the early part of my marketing career in customer marketing and product marketing roles at Microsoft. At the time, most organizations did not have a dedicated sales enablement team and product marketing served as the bridge between marketing and sales. I was introduced to HubSpot when I moved back to the Boston area. I saw a great opportunity to join and create a sales enablement team, which allowed me to leverage my previous experience and grow a new team and discipline at a company that believed in "Smarketing" (collaboration between marketing and sales).

BRIAN: Tell me about your experience having worked with a couple of sales orgs previously and what kind of product marketing work you did. What did that look like?

DEBBIE: I'd like to use an example to help shed light on the relationship between product marketing and enabling a sales team. At Microsoft, I worked on the launch of Office 2010 for the commercial side of the business. It was my job to work with the product team to understand the new features they were building, translate that into what business value those features would have for customers, create content for the global sales team to use in their sales calls, and train the sellers on how to have effective conversations.

BRIAN: What sort of perspective do you have on where the sales enablement function itself came from and if it's even been around long enough to have evolved?

DEBBIE: I think "sales enablement" has become quite a buzzword and a lot of people define it differently. In my opinion, the lead-to-customer conversion rate is the business metric that should guide all sales enablement activities. The job of a sales enablement professional is to provide buyers with helpful information throughout the buyer's journey. There are two sides to that: (1) Understanding what research a buyer is doing on his own and providing content there, and (2) empowering the sales team with content and training to meet the buyer where they are.

The way that I think that things have changed is that people have so much more access to information these days, meaning buyers are more independent and empowered. Analysts at Gartner and Forrester have quoted that people do over two-thirds of their research on their own before they ever talk to a sales rep. Therefore, it's important to think about the buyer's journey holistically, and not just about the role of the sales rep. I think it's the job of the sales enablement team to provide interesting and helpful content at all of the buyer's touch points.

BRIAN: Like you said, it's not about product training or helping solely with product launches. Sales enablement is also about understanding how to strategically influence or even control part of the message that is out there in the world as someone goes through a buyer's journey, which is critical considering how much research buyers do *without* sales reps today.

DEBBIE: Totally. An example of how that has played out at HubSpot is related to customer advocacy. We always had a customer reference program, but recognized that buyers were more often considering product reviews, social media conversations, and less formal references during their evaluation. So, we turned up the dial on our advocacy efforts and educated the sales team on how to leverage them.

BRIAN: How did HubSpot decide that it was time to build out a sales enablement team?

DEBBIE: I'll talk about my first project. I worked for HubSpot as a contractor for one month before I joined full time.

My job was to conduct a buyer's journey study. HubSpot had clearly defined personas but nobody had ever dug in and asked, "What are people doing when they're not talking to our sales team? Which sources of information are they looking at during their evaluation process? What was their experience was like working with our sales team? What are the things that will ultimately drive their decision?" The completion of that project answered those questions and uncovered the need for a sales enablement team. It basically wrote my job description and then—overall—our team's charter in terms of the different activities that we were missing out on.

BRIAN: A couple of things you touched on I want to go into a little bit more. Mostly around data and people, just understanding how you went about getting access to the information you needed so you could understand whether the sales team was helpful or were they more traditional, let's say, maybe pushy. How do you identify it? Or, for example, coming back to the point when you realized the need to find trigger events, how did you access information?

DEBBIE: Sure. I think there are two aspects to your question. The first is how I gathered the data in the study; and then, how we executed the vision.

The buyer's journey study had two phases: the first phase was qualitative and the second phase was quantitative. For the qualitative study, I created a discussion guide that dug into the buyer's purchase process and stuck to very open-ended questions to avoid leading them with any preconceived notions. I picked a subset of customers who had newly onboarded with HubSpot so that their purchasing decision was very fresh in their head. Then I chose a subset of potential customers who had chosen not to purchase HubSpot either because they had decided not to buy anything or they went with a competitor. It was equally important to understand why they didn't purchase HubSpot and how those buyers were different. I did 20 to 30 phone interviews that allowed me to shape my hypotheses. Then, I created a quantitative survey that I sent out to a much bigger volume of buyers to validate the hypotheses. The respondents simply answered an online survey, which gave us the numbers to analyze to complement the story we had from the phone conversations.

In terms of building out the team, I think there are a few things that I always look for in terms of someone who'll make a good sales enablement marketer. Number one is that they have to understand how a sales team ticks, even if they've never worked with one before. That's one thing that's essential because sometimes these two groups can conflict, but you have to find the people who will approach the differences with curiosity and interest. The second piece is that they have to have great written and verbal communication skills. Salespeople tend to be short on time and short on attention span. You have to know how to communicate a message in a way that can catch their attention, that will matter to them, that will motivate them. I think everyone who's on our team has that skill set. We have to be able to go deep, deep in the product, deep in the marketing and really understand the guts of how things work, but then pull out the little nuggets that the salespeople need to know.

BRIAN: What are the things that a business leader should be looking for to understand, "Aha, now we need a sales enablement function or we need to set it up more properly"?

DEBBIE: As marketers, we always think about our marketing funnel and the most important thing is that you first have a healthy top of the funnel. You should be generating the right volume of leads that support your sales team. They should be very good quality leads.

Once you feel like you have that healthy top of the funnel, it's time to think about investing more effort in terms of having marketers help support the sales team. If you have a strong lead flow but can improve your lead-to-customer conversion, that's when it makes sense to start a sales enablement team.

Historically, most marketers viewed their job as generating leads and then walking away, but if you think about it, marketers have such a strong skill set that can help in terms of converting customers. It shouldn't be sales' job alone to do that. You should draw on both sales talent and marketing talents to work together to talk to customers.

BRIAN: Who owns it [sales enablement]? And how do you ultimately interface with general groups like the marketing team, the sales team, operations, and so forth?

It seems like you would need to be everywhere at once.

DEBBIE: This is an ongoing debate. Where does sales enablement team sit in the organization? Does it sit in marketing or in sales? I think it depends on your company and views on the role of the team.

At HubSpot, our team originally sat within marketing. We are a very content-driven company and the core skill sets of the team belonged in marketing. It also helped us bridge the gap between the two organizations by physically sitting with sales but organizationally sitting with marketing and going to marketing team meetings. Since then, we divided the sales enablement responsibilities between product marketing, field marketing, and sales operations. Sales operations now owns all of the processes and training.

BRIAN: If you would have liked me to ask one question, what would that be?

DEBBIE: It would be about the measurement component of sales enablement. My advice would be to use your lead-to-customer conversion rate as your north star. Think about every project you take on. Is that going to help move people who are already existing leads or who are already aware of your company? If not, then that project probably goes to other people in marketing.

Measurement is one of the things that keeps me up at night. There is more technology coming onto the market that helps with this, which I think is going to be very important. Historically, marketing and sales could measure the number of leads generated and revenue closed, but it was hard to see what was happening in between.

BRIAN: When we take a peak around the corner and think about the future, what does the next three to five years look like? Maybe it's around something like what technologies you would like to see or how you see the sales enablement team or function evolving? Any thoughts on what's next for the sales enablement world?

DEBBIE: I think that the evolution of sales and marketing software is what will really shape the next chapter of sales enablement. The tools will provide more buyer-friendly experiences, efficiency through automation, and insights through analytics.

I really think that the next evolution in this area is all summed up in what we call Smarketing. It's all about bridging sales and marketing together in the same technology as well as having those two teams work together. I feel very fortunate. I've never met another company like HubSpot where the sales team and the marketing team get along so well. It's really, really special and so I'm really looking forward to the day when we'd use the same technology to help one another, our prospects, and our customers.

Part 4: Building a Sales Operations Team to Set Up Growth

AN INTERVIEW WITH DAVID MCNEIL, VP GLOBAL SALES OPERATIONS (2014–2016), HUBSPOT[4]
December 2015. Edited for length and clarity.

BRIAN: David, let's start with how you came to HubSpot. What led up to you running our global sales operations and strategy team, starting in early 2014?

DAVID: Before I joined HubSpot, I was running Sales Development (Enterprise Development Reps) for all of Americas at Salesforce for about two and a half years. My team was responsible for driving new business pipeline through traditional outbound calling tactics. It was a phenomenal point in my career. I had a great time and learned a lot about scaling hypergrowth sales organizations, but for family medical reasons, I had to move from San Francisco to Boston. With that move, I decided that it was in the best interest of my family to work with a local company where I could commit to both the company and my family needs.

I was introduced to the CEO of HubSpot, Brian Halligan, when I was assessing the market and local companies. The first conversation was pretty much a whiteboard session sketching out various concepts of sales operations, how companies scale, and how operational excellence drives the success of the sales team. We finished the meeting and I thought, "That was fun! This is the kind of work I enjoy doing and we both understand the strategic value of this kind of work. We should do this."

That's how I ended up here. The sales ops role itself was pretty unique for me. Previously in my career, I led various sales organizations, and while I had always worked closely with sales ops, I never owned that as my sole function. However, I understood the value of data, process, and operational rigor and always leaned heavily into these capabilities in order to scale my team's success.

BRIAN: Having led the sales ops function here for almost two years now, what goes into defining that team's role and responsibilities?

DAVID: Over the last 10 years the SaaS industry has really embraced and evolved the concept of sales ops. The industry figured out how essential it is to build a hyper-growth sales organization, especially businesses that have lower average selling prices and need operational rigor for the sales machine to work. In contrast, when I was at Bank of America, sales ops was a super tactical reporting, data management, and analytics function, and it still is at most companies today. There are a lot of people that do a lot of data analysis but the reports these functions provide don't always offer strategic value and are not fully connected back to the business. Then it is up to sales managers, often with little time and analytical experience, to interpret the data to figure out what the actionable takeaways might be. While almost every manager today understands the importance of data in terms of planning and directing their teams, only a few understand the importance of data well enough to incorporate it in the day-to-day responsibilities of running their team. This is where sales ops can step in, moving from what used to be a pure support and "order-taker" reporting type function to a strategic partner that can interpret the data for you and make it actionable for sales managers and reps.

As an example, when I began working more closely with sales ops at Bank of America, they helped me completely rethink our business. We started to connect dots that hadn't been connected before. We started segmenting our customers differently based on their needs and launched a new telesales organization to meet the needs of small- to medium-size businesses that were not getting the attention they needed from the in-field sales reps. We provided these new telesales reps with the processes, tools, and resources they needed to drive consistent and repeatable value to these previously "unserved" segment of customers. That led to tremendous success in retaining these customers and new growth opportunities in various parts of the cash management and credit business that people just didn't see before. That was the beauty of transitioning sales ops from a support function to a strategic business partner role—they helped us find hidden gems of productivity in our business, which allowed us to scale and grow more effectively during a challenging time when the bank was dealing with the 2008 banking crisis.

BRIAN: What were some of the things that you and Brian Halligan talked about during that whiteboard session to make you realize there was a strong need for a sales operations team at HubSpot?

DAVID: When I joined HubSpot's sales organization, it was growing and doing well. That said, a SaaS business typically requires a lot of hiring. As you lay the groundwork to grow a SaaS business ten times over in, say, five years, you need a repeatable and consistent set of hiring, onboarding and sales processes in place. You just can't do it without having the right operational rigor, infrastructure and team in place.

So, from that first conversation with Halligan, I was excited knowing HubSpot was already at this critical pre-IPO point, was well respected in the industry, and had proven its product by truly solving its customers' needs. It was by no means a fledgling business trying to figure out product-market fit. HubSpot was at a critical crossroads and knew that to grow tenfold in the next five years—or to even have a shot at it—it needed consistent hiring profiles, great insight into its own business operations, clear systems in place to realize that, and a well-defined sales process for new team members to follow as they joined the growing organization. We also needed to make sure we had clear alignment between other upstream and downstream organizations.

Here's an example of this alignment playing out in practice: Think about all the co-dependencies we have with the marketing team and what happens if we're not perfectly coordinated. If we were planning to enter new markets with an inbound sales team but didn't have that market primed with lead flow, our ability to be successful would be extremely limited. For marketing to be successful they need the foresight into sales' perspective on the go-to-market strategy, at least six to twelve months ahead of time to hire a local marketing manager, localize content, and build out market specific campaigns. That's one of the key roles of the sales ops team—to bridge, in this instance, the gap between sales and marketing.

If the sales ops team does its job well, then the marketing team ends up seeding a new market with consistent inbound lead flow instead of our sales team trying to develop a completely unknown territory with traditional outbound tactics. Getting those relationships to a state of full collaboration across the broader organization is what makes sales ops not only really exciting to me, but incredibly powerful in any organization trying to grow quickly.

Brian: Hearing that example, I think it's clear that there's a misconception of what sales ops not only can do, but *should* do. There's this misconception that sales ops is much more of a support role and takes a backseat to the rest of the business. But, at least from what you just described, sales ops are more like drivers in the business and less like passengers. You're in the front seat and you're saying, "No, this is where we're going. We've got the navigation. We've got the map. Everyone follow us this way." Do you agree?

DAVID: I totally agree. If, for example, you know you need to build a superhighway instead of a country road, the way you're going to approach the problem is very different. Our job is to build a superhighway for HubSpot. I try to think about the things we're doing today and how that lays the framework for where we need to be in 6 months, 12 months, 18 months, or 3 years from now.

The head of sales ops job is to always think ahead, not to focus too much on the current month or quarter. If we're doing our job right, we already know what this quarter will bring. So, instead, we spend our time checking in to make sure that nothing is happening that we didn't already anticipate. We're looking at the data coming out of the business to see if there's a pothole forming or a structural weakness that maybe we hadn't anticipated that will impact us in future quarters.

BRIAN: For a leader whose business might be growing rapidly, what advice might you have for them on determining the right time to build a sales ops team?

DAVID: I think it's all about what you're trying to do. How much change are you trying to induce within your own business? Are you building a small business, or are you trying to build a high-growth business? How much is your business model evolving? Is the focus on new business growth and/or retention and cross-sell? If you're about to introduce a potentially significant amount of change, you might need to rethink your go-to-market strategy; or, if you're trying to build scale for hypergrowth, then you need to staff a sales ops team as early as possible to make sure you're set up for sustainable success.

Another great example is a friend of mine who runs a sales ops team *really* well. He has three people on his team and that's it. It's a $15 million business. He's the EVP of sales and head of sales ops. The business is going through a lot of change, shifting from a hardware business to a software company focused on connected devices in the Internet of Things (IoT) world. That's a very different business model and market than the one they're currently in today, yet he sees the opportunity and so he spending a disproportionate amount of his team's time and focus on evolving the company go-to-market strategy and sales process to prepare them for the future.

Instead of focusing his time on current sales, he's spending his time crafting the business case for it, making the connection points, figuring out how to move into that new space. If he does his job right, it takes the business from where it is today to growing by a factor or three to five times revenue. They just haven't had that potential in the past. By thinking and acting like a sales ops strategist and go-to-market strategist, he's helping take the business in an entirely different direction. However, he can't forgo current sales either, so he is conflicted and his time vacillates back and forth between short-term and long-term needs. Having a person that is solely focused and dedicated in that area of sales strategy and ops would help him manage to current business needs and expectations, while also preparing the business for the important changes ahead.

So, to answer your question, I don't think it's a matter of current company size or stage. It's really a matter of where you're trying to go and how fast you're looking to change. And arguably, it's never a waste of time to have a person, or small group of people, thinking strategically about where the business needs to be in the next 6 months, 12 months or even 3 years.

BRIAN: David, let's talk about your team for a little bit. As you thought about building up HubSpot's strategy and operations team, what type of talent were you looking for? And if you could throw everything away and start from scratch again, how would you change your approach to building the team?

DAVID: Out of the gate, one of the few things I got right was the types of folks I hired and the team size. It was incredible, the talent that was in place when I got here. They were all very smart and motivated, but they were more technically oriented—either from the systems perspective, or from a data science perspective. What I really needed was a small team of people that had an understanding of data but who could also apply it to solving near and long-term problems, evolving our sales processes and facilitating change.

To find the right profile of a sales ops person at HubSpot, it was a unique and frankly difficult mix of skills to find. My criteria was to find someone who can wear a business strategy hat, who is a creative problem solver, who is a strong communicator, very good at cross-team collaboration, but who can also do complex data analysis. I really needed that balance and I was very fortunate to find folks who had that experience working at well-respected consulting companies with three to five years of experience. Their consulting background gave them exposure to very different situations. They all had a high "figure-it-out factor," working with executives and business leaders to solve complex problems at a rapid pace, and they had exceptional communication and collaboration skills to drive change.

As I evolved the team, I added a few folks who were previously in the sales ops function at different companies. They were all working at companies that weren't growing at the same rate as HubSpot, but they had lots of technical experience and they understood the reporting needs of a business. I also hired folks with varying skill levels. One of my team members outside of our US headquarters came from a big technology company and was working in a sales ops capacity at a management level. Another young gentleman, who turned out to be a phenomenal hire, came in as an entry-level analyst straight out of school. My goal was to build a balanced team with a mix of skills that could learn from each other.

However, what I (and the broader team) was missing was historical context around HubSpot's business specifically. I had built a brand new team, all super smart, ready and motivated, but they didn't know HubSpot. Because they hadn't been through a planning cycle at HubSpot they weren't able to anticipate the needs of the business and understand what planning potholes we would run into. To fill this gap, I was fortunate enough to recruit somebody from our finance team to help. She was a phenomenal addition to the team because she had over two years of experience working at the company, had a ton of credibility with the leadership team, and had developed several of our financial models, so she intimately understood the drivers and levers in our business. That was the perfect complement for us at the time and really helped us excel as a team.

BRIAN: Did you and HubSpot's Chief Sales Officer, Hunter Madeley [*SVP Sales at time of interview*], talk about how you would go to market, so to speak, together internally? I feel like that is potentially a major pothole that other companies might run into. How did you make it work here?

DAVID: Interestingly enough we didn't but I think we immediately complemented each other well. When we came into HubSpot, we started within two weeks of each other. We had a lot of work to do, so we partnered with each other in some areas, but we both had immediate things we needed to get done. We set up regular routines and touched base along the way. Even though we didn't formally discuss how to go to market together and define clear roles and responsibilities, we built a relationship and a mutual appreciation for each other's skills. I think it happened much more naturally and organically than either of us had planned.

I'd say if there's only one thing I would have done differently, it would have been spending more time upfront planning and coordinating between myself (as head of sales ops) and Hunter (head of sales). We were so focused on having an impact in each of our roles, we did not intentionally spend enough time upfront together. We had to figure it all out behind the scenes, but we kept the face to the organization as if we were this dynamic duo wrapped in one. We probably weren't as in sync as we could have been if we had just spent a bit more time together or grabbed a meal together once a week to brainstorm and make sure we were aligned. If I had to do one thing over, I would have spent more time upfront understanding some of his drivers and perspectives, to make sure we were coming to a shared point of view together, faster.

BRIAN: Is there anything that really stands out in your mind as to what allowed for some of your early success running sales ops at HubSpot?

DAVID: For me, I did my due diligence in the hiring process so I knew what the big rocks were and the key challenges we faced when I joined the business. But I also came in with a preconceived idea of what the solutions might be. I came in with these ideas based on my previous experiences and levers I thought we needed to pull to grow faster.

In other words, a "needs assessment," is step one in everything. It was really understanding HubSpot's true needs, the problems the company was trying to solve, and the guardrails for us to stay within. The existing strength of HubSpot's business both now and at that time—consistent, significant, and predictable inbound lead flow and an inbound sales methodology—is really what makes the business run and tick and why it has been successful to date, so we didn't want to screw that up. Instead of completely changing our model based on my previous telesales and outbound experience, I worked with the team to leverage our inbound strengths and simply nudge the business in the direction it needed to go in the future with deeper segmentation, territory planning, and standardization of more disciplined onboarding and sales processes.

The last area for me, which was almost the most important, was in the way I organized the sales operations team and set them up for success. Instead of organizing the team around functions (for example, somebody runs reporting and somebody else runs sales processes design) we aligned each person to a business segment. This allowed each person on the team to become a true business partner to a sales leader of the business and truly understand that business's needs. We had four or five different segments at the time and we were expanding rapidly internationally, so this helped us make sure we understood the nuances and differences of the various segments and markets. We also had each person own at least one global reporting and/or process function, which drove cross-team collaboration and dependences.

That was probably the number one factor that gave the team the credibility they needed to build trust on the front lines with sales managers and reps. For sales ops to be impactful, it needs to be focused on front line enablement and finding early successes, then connecting slowly moving teams to a more constant and repeatable process. That was one of the key missing elements, particularly as we looked at how sales ops was aligned at HubSpot initially.

Historically, when I worked with sales ops teams that were organized around various core reporting and process functions, it didn't work well. They weren't aligned to a specific need of the business unit. When sales ops teams are organized this way, they can't anticipate how changes will impact one business unit over another. They would rollout changes and realize they had low adoption, so they'd say, "Oh, I have to go tweak this for the small business segment. All right, I did that. Now I'm going to go work on the channel business. I'm going to go do that. Now I'm going to go work on the corporate business segment." But when you're doing that you're constantly tweaking and modifying poorly designed processes to make them work and you end up with a set of reports, systems and business processes that don't help the business scale over time.

BRIAN: If you were to give some advice to other peers, like yourself, or other CEOs or sales leaders that were looking to set up the sales operations function, what insights might you offer?

DAVID: Where to start? Again, the first step is to understand what problem you're trying to solve. Are you trying to tweak, evolve, or completely transform your business? Are you trying to scale it to a 3–5x rate? Something else? The problem you're trying to solve will determine the type of team and sales ops organization you need to build. If you're looking to scale an organization 3–5x, you want somebody that has a good strategy background but has equal understanding of what it means to run sales and they should really, really enjoy creating sustainable, repeatable processes.

Second is to find the best and most talented people possible. There are so many really smart people out there that get excited when they hear about this type of job, especially when they realize it's going to affect the way a business is run and performs in a positive way. When you recruit talent, you should find people that really care deeply about the impact they can have on a day in the life of a customer, of a frontline sales rep, of a partner, or of a sales manager. Go find people that enjoy solving complex problems guided by data, but are equally comfortable rolling up their sleeves to understand what it takes to implement and change behavior on the front lines. Get them to talk about their experiences from a human perspective, or a customer perspective, or a partner perspective. If you can find those people with strategy, data analysis, and business process experience and instill in them that commitment and passion to solving for the customer, sales rep, manager, and company, you'll be unstoppable.

Part 5

The Future of Sales and the Sales Profession

Chapter **11**

The Future of Sales
An Epilogue

by Derek Wyszynski, board advisor at SalesTribe and CEO of RealSalesAdvice

For this final chapter, I asked modern sales expert and sales futurist Derek Wyszynski to take the reins. While I do have my own opinions on what the future holds for the sales profession, I thought it would more valuable for you to hear an outside perspective. For those of you who don't know Derek, you should. He's a brilliant sales leader and author. In particular, I encourage you to read his LinkedIn post titled "John Henry the Salesperson," which was the very article that inspired me to ask him to write this chapter. I hope you enjoy reading his take on what the future of sales may hold for us all.

■ ■ ■

LOCATION: San Juan, Puerto Rico

YEAR: 2037

On August 27, 2037, 600 feet above the corner of Avenida Juan Ponce de Leon and Avenue De Diego, Pat's eyes burst opened as the entire known universe was instantly filled with the sound of music.

Rolling out of a canvas hammock, purchased on Prime Day 2035 for $1,359.00, Pat hit the floor. It was 7:00 a.m. and the soundtrack from that 72-year-old movie played in Pat's aural implants—Julie Andrews's soaring rendition of "The Hills Are Alive" from Pat's personal cloud storage repository.

With a flick of an earlobe, Pat made Julie Andrews and her living hills fade away. Pat's field of vision was overlaid with a customized augmented reality (AR) home screen—the Intel corneal implants seemed to be taking last night's upgrade well. No more blurry text. Pat blinked and looked up—a calendar appeared. Pat had three meetings today. Busy day.

Walking five steps to the window, Pat reflected. At 450 square feet, Pat's apartment was among the largest in the building. Many families were living in much smaller apartments. Pat had no family to speak of, so in this apartment, it was just Pat. Lots of room for one person. *If I had a nickel for every evil eye I get from the neighbors in the elevator*, Pat thought, *I'd have a shit-ton of nickels.*

Pat was on the receiving end of those evil eyes mostly because the neighbors were jealous. And with good reason. Unlike most human beings living in 2037, Pat's survival wasn't contingent on Universal Basic Income. That paltry $5,000 a week that the government deposited into every citizen's debit account wasn't even something Pat touched.

Pat had a "job." And that job gave Pat "expendable income"; ergo, Pat had luxurious living accommodations, far exceeding what the neighbors were accustomed to themselves.

Pat looked out at the city of San Juan and thought of what Grandfather used to say—some quote from an old TV show— "There are 8 million stories in the Naked City." Pat laughed. Grandfather's old show was about New York—now a city-state with more than 40 million people, half of them children. San Juan—hovering around 4 million people (3 million children, last count)—had enough stories of its own.

And most of them were sad.

But there weren't any people in the window—none of the 4 million residents made an appearance. All Pat saw was the San

Juan skyline, full of buildings just like the one Pat was standing in. And in those buildings, were people—most likely looking out at the skyline themselves.

But that wasn't all. Pat also saw huge metal cranes and enormous "hover barges" with big mechanical doodads—all to build more buildings. But the thing Pat saw the most of was bots. Lots of bots. *Busy bots building big buildings,* Pat thought.

Just 20 years before, 600 feet below the very spot Pat stood this morning, a quaint little liquor store (*Wow, imagine drinking liquor,* Pat thought) stood on this corner. Now there was a 75-story building, housing tens of thousands of people, most of them miserable.

Pat turned from the window and grabbed something gray and squarish from the shelf. Like millions of other of Sanjuaneros this morning, Pat undressed, then unfolded and stepped into an Amazon portable sonic shower. A date with Chris was on Pat's schedule for Friday night, and Pat saw no reason to waste any of the "three-gallon hot water ration" before then.

"Shower," Pat spoke.

Within 1.5 seconds, a billion invisible sonic waves silently pummeled Pat's body, knocking off dirt, grime, and the detritus of daily human existence.

It was a hell of an invention. People like Pat didn't exactly know the science, but they knew without it, civilization would have crumbled after the worldwide Fresh Water Crisis of 2028. In less than 10 years, there were 15 billion sonic showers in use around the world—historian bots on CNNMSNFOX said it rivaled the "smartphone" revolution of 2007 to 2020.

Pat—as did most of the people that used one daily—hated it. Yes it "cleaned" them, literally and scientifically. But no one ever really "felt" clean. There was just something about hot, soapy water and the act of washing oneself that made a human being "feel clean."

But hot showers were for rich people—like Pat. And this sonic shower was better than half the world dying of thirst just so rich people could sprinkle a little hot water on their ass every day. At least Pat thought so. Again, Pat was lucky—most of the neighbors probably hadn't had a hot water shower in at least a decade.

During this "shower," Pat's eyes shifted up and left, and the AR screen scrolled the text of the first calendar appointment for the day.

Contract Negotiation—Alice-Bot.9283 from Datadyne—11 a.m.–11:15 a.m.

Yeesh, Pat thought, *15 whole minutes for this meeting? What the hell were they negotiating? The Magna Carta? And Alice-Bot.9283 was a ball-busting bot. Pat's last negotiation with her was scheduled for 8 minutes and ran almost 12!*

Twelve minutes of my life I'll never get back, Pat thought while turning 360 degrees in the "shower."

Pat finished "washing" and stepped off the pad, folding the shower and placing it back on the shelf. Walking the seven steps to the living area/clothes closet/kitchen, Pat stifled a chuckle—yes, complaining about Alice-Bot.9283 was ridiculous. Pat's company was one of the biggest employers in the entire State of Puerto Rico—over 125 human beings were gainfully employed, full time! *And I'm lucky to be one of them,* Pat thought.

Getting dressed, Pat called out for breakfast—the avocado toast and triple-shot caramel latte would be ready in four minutes. Friends laughed that Pat drank something so old fashioned—coworkers gave endless grief that Pat waited "in line" with all the "blue hairs" at the old Starbucks in the San Juan historical district for coffee—but Pat preferred caffeine in drinkable form and not in the nasal mist form that was all the rage today.

Dressed and now eating breakfast, Pat swiped eyes right and accepted the Alice Bot meeting. The second meeting that showed up on Pat's AR was no better than the first—another ball-buster bot and another 12 minutes shot to hell.

But that's the job, Pat thought, *and someone who's human has gotta do it.* Again, eyes swiped right.

It was amazing, and more than a bit ridiculous to Pat that there were any jobs anymore. The bot revolution of the 2020s really decimated the worldwide labor industry—advancements in computing power and algorithms and all that techie stuff no human really understands anymore really took off after the invention of the BBot (BrainBot) neural programming language in 2020.

For the first time, code was written for a bot that passed the Turing test—making human interaction with a bot nondiscernible from a human to human interaction. While revolutionary in itself, that was the same year IBM perfected writing data on an atomic level (basically writing 1s and 0s on atoms) so that Turing-tested code could use almost unlimited storage for data—reaching *far* past the human brain capacity of 2.5 petabytes.

It was a perfect storm. *Just like the old movie*, Pat thought. And just like the movie, Pat knew that very few people would survive.

Sooner than anyone could even imagine, everyone from doctors and lawyers to janitors and food service workers were quickly replaced by bots. Even coders who wrote the original bot code were replaced—as it turned out, self-aware bots with unlimited brain capacity wrote better code that humans clickity-clacking on keyboards while eating Cheetos and drinking Red Bull.

Pat knew North American history was replete with instances of citizens ranting about "jobs"—there were not enough of them or there wasn't enough compensation for the jobs they did have. But most of all, people throughout history had ranted about how "other people" were coming to take their jobs and that the jobs North Americans needed were being shipped to other people in other countries. The ranting had permeated popular culture, global economics, and national politics. Well, it turned out, after all that sound and fury, those ranting were half right—someone had "finally" come to "take the jobs." But no borders were crossed, and no jobs were shipped. Just a few people in Silicon Valley, a million gallons of caffeine, billions in venture capital, some electricity, a few 1s and 0s and "poof," the jobs were gone.

World governments scrambled to meet the need—jobless people needed income, so Universal Basic Income became international practice. And for a year or two it was nice—really nice—like the entire human race was on vacation. Because production was at an all-time high, everyone had some form of income, and there was a lot of stuff to buy.

But like all vacations, there comes a time when you have to pay the hotel bill. No one in Silicon Valley had ever thought about what people would do with all that free time if they didn't have to work. A few years was all it took for them, *and the rest of us*, Pat thought, to find out.

The worldwide population exploded. In five years, it doubled. Then the water crisis.

Pat shook that thought away *We got through those years*, he thought. *It was rough, but we made it.*

Far enough away from the bad years, Pat could say that the funniest thing about it all was that of all the jobs bots could do well, there was one silly job they still couldn't do.

And that's the job Pat had.

It seemed bots could be programmed to do all kinds of things—write a legal brief, extract a bullet from a person's body—even write fiction stories and act on television. But for some reason, no one—not even the bots themselves—could program a bot to successfully buy something for someone.

Not that anyone didn't try to change that. Pat remembered over the years that Amazon, Google, Facebook, Microsoft, and HubSpot (and a million smaller companies) all came out with shopper bots. The basic idea was the human could plug in all the needs or wants they had and then let the bot search for the best "whatever" you needed or wanted. And it was an abject failure. Coders could program a bot to do open heart surgery on a seven-month-old fetus—but try programming it to buy a canary-yellow bedspread and all hell broke loose, because the bots couldn't ever be programmed to make a purchase the bot itself deemed unnecessary or illogical.

Like most educated people who had graduated the tenth grade, Pat knew that if human history showed anything at all, it showed that unnecessary or illogical were two things human beings did both exceptionally well and incredibly often. And in a cruel twist of fate, as if the universe were an old situational comedy based on some incredibly ridiculous premise—like seven castaways trapped on an island or six underemployed friends living in the most expensive city in the world—it just so happened that the economic engine on which the entire planet seemed to depend was built firmly on unnecessary or illogical purchases made by human beings.

So, that was Pat's job. Not choosing bedspreads—but buying stuff and things for companies.

Pat was a professional buyer—working with companies and organizations to help them buy whatever bots or tech or stuff or things they needed to do whatever the hell it was they were doing. Pat spent the entire four-hour workday demoing, trialing, and testing stuff to see whether it solved whatever problem a company was experiencing. Pat dealt with sales bots and demo bots and negotiation bots all day long.

Pat had a full-time job, 20 hours of work a week—and if the price for a paycheck that didn't say "State of Puerto Rico" on it was meeting with sales bots, then Pat would "swipe right" all day long.

But having accepted the first two meetings, it was the last meeting on the calendar, the one not yet accepted, that was gnawing at Pat.

Devin—Retirement Sendoff—5:45 P.M.–6:10 P.M., O'Shaughnessy's Public House

That's right—Devin was retiring, Pat reflected with a blink. The calendar asked:

"To accept this meeting swipe eyes right."

Devin—*the entire remaining human sales force for Data-dyne*—was retiring. Pat knew Devin was the last of a dying—hell, a dead—breed. Twenty years ago, Devin had been hired by Datadyne as a salesperson. Pat and Devin worked together for years—save for the mandatory international pause in "non-water"-related work during the "bad times"—but even after that long relationship, Pat had been forced to request that a bot handle his account a few years back. Devin was nice enough, but Pat had tired of the "human" content and "organic" thought leadership—that stuff wasn't going to keep Pat employed for long.

That's not to say Devin was not a great sales*person*—Pat knew that Devin was the pinnacle of human achievement in that regard. The problem was that didn't really mean much compared to the average sales bots being coded in 2037.

Chewing the last few bits of toast, Pat thought about that term *salesperson*. In the bot revolution of the 2020s, one of the first jobs to go was the traditional business salesperson. When Pat first started out as a buyer, older, more seasoned, buyers would tell stories of "salespeople" they worked with in the late teens and early 20s. They were all the same story: some guy or gal, sending an email asking for something. *The digital version of holding out a hat*, Pat thought.

Pat even heard stories of salespeople calling buyers on the phone (the phone!) to ask for a meeting. Out of the blue, with no idea about whom they were reaching out to—Pat finished the toast and laughed . . . *what were they thinking?*

Drinking the latte, Pat also remembered there was something in those stories about "quotas" and "commissions" and something called a "sales process" that those old-timers mentioned. But Pat couldn't remember what they meant by those terms. In 2037, those words meant as much to Pat as "telegraph," "postcard," and "college"—just historical terms from a bygone era.

But Devin hadn't been like the old-timey salespeople in those stories. Finishing the coffee, Pat remembered meeting Devin for the first time all those years ago. Pat had been searching the Internet (*with a keyboard and a screen*) for some business software. But as a new buyer, Pat really had no idea what was truly "needed."

Pat wasn't a software expert—Pat was a buyer. So, Pat did what all buyers did—research.

That's when Pat ran across Devin's written content on some old social media site. It had been incredibly helpful—informing and educating Pat on what needed to be purchased and why. Pat started researching and reading a lot of Devin's content. Some of the content was text, some video, some AR—and Pat found Devin to be a great resource. So, Pat reached out to Devin, and after a 20-minute virtual meeting, Devin became Pat's salesperson.

And Devin did it all—not just content. Devin was an expert demonstrator and presenter, always perfecting a customized approach to all different types of buyer and user personas (when there were still users.)

And customer success? Devin took that on as well. As human salespeople evolved into customer experience engineers, Devin was on the forefront. Always one step ahead. *Until the steps ran out*, Pat thought, looking at the words now flashing on the AR calendar:

"To accept this meeting swipe eyes right."

Devin had been a great resource over the years. Pat used Devin's insight and knowledge to make a lot of purchases, purchases to the tune of a few billion dollars, in fact, all because of Devin. Until a couple of years ago.

First, Pat had noticed Devin couldn't keep up with the content—versions and releases and new products were coming out daily—sometimes hourly. Bots could write, record, produce, and publish content instantly—as soon as a new product or version was released. Devin, on the other hand, took almost a full day to create or curate new content to share with buyers.

That left almost no time to demo, practice good customer success, or even negotiate. Pat had heard from a colleague at another company that Devin was working nonstop and still falling behind.

Jobs were hard to come by. And if Pat wasn't buying the right things, the company would give Pat's job to someone else. And then it's goodbye luxury apartment—hello 100 square feet and Universal Basic Income.

Pat looked at the blinking message and remembered that Devin had been pretty understanding. *I need my job,* Pat had told Devin, *and I can't wait for you to digest, write or create content.* So, Pat asked for a bot—Devin was upset but said it wasn't surprising.

Devin had actually said, "No hard feelings."

Pat thought about that last conversation. Devin had been able to hold out longer than most. There were a handful of human salespeople left in the world. Now, there was one less.

"To accept this meeting swipe eyes right."

Pat's eyes swiped left.

Nope, I'm not going. I haven't spoken to Devin in a couple years, and honestly, it's too sad. Besides, I don't owe Devin anything.

Pat sat down in the work chair and said, "Work." The AR schedule disappeared and the entire universe came alive in Pat's eyes and ears. There were billions of bits of content and insight ready to be found out there—and thanks to sales bots, the content that Pat may use in a few minutes to decide what to buy might not even be written, recorded, or published yet.

Pat's eyelids flicked twice—and Pat's purchase objective for the day was at last revealed.

It was time.

On August 27, 2037, 600 feet above the corner of Avenida Juan Ponce de Leon and Avenue De Diego, and less than 19 minutes after waking up, Pat said the word "Search," and started on a buyer's journey—alone.

■ ■ ■

Is this what the future holds for us as salespeople? Is it all "here's your hat, here's your coat, what's your hurry?" I don't know.

You can probably tell I am a child of the late seventies who was raised on dystopian movies on late night TV, like *Soylent Green*, *The Omega Man*, and *Planet of the Apes*—which begs the question: *Did Charlton Heston make any non-dystopian movies that decade?*

Today it seems we've come full circle—you can't throw a rock in public without hitting a person that's glued to their "content viewing appliance of choice," binge-watching a zombie apocalypse show, a vampire conspiracy movie trilogy, or some other "it's the end of the world as we know it" entertainment.

So maybe you feel you can ignore those parts of my little fiction. Chalk it up to some guy trying to be too clever. Maybe artificial intelligence won't ever be realized. Maybe you can bet against innovation and technology. Maybe you think there will always be a need for salespeople, right?

But there's one thing I don't think you can bet against and that's human nature. What do I mean?

Well, here's some nonfiction for you. Did you know that in 2018:

- Some VPs of sales buy houses that they find on RedFin or Zillow?
- Some major account executives buy cars on TrueCar or Carfax?
- Some sales development reps buy refrigerators and TVs and gaming consoles on Amazon?

Of course, you did.

Everyone who has a job in B2B sales today buys this way. They use the Internet for research, either to winnow down their choices or to actually purchase a product or service.

People don't buy anything without going on the Internet. If you go somewhere new for lunch without looking at Yelp, you're probably (1) an alien from another planet or (2) my parents. It's the age we live in. It's how we buy.

We stream movies on Netflix while in our underwear, because we choose comfort over putting on pants to drive to Blockbuster. We read books on our Kindles, because we'd rather download our books than put on pants and go to Borders. We buy our electronics on Amazon, because we'd rather get same day shipping than put on pants and drive down to Circuit City. There's a common thread here—and it's not our common hatred of pants. It's that we are making a choice to engage in a personal buying process without the aid of a salesperson.

And now, those three companies I mentioned (Blockbuster, Borders, and Circuit City) don't exist anymore because we made that choice. Did you also know:

♦ 19,500 employees lost their jobs when Borders closed?
♦ 30,000 employees lost their jobs when Circuit City went bankrupt?
♦ 84,300 employees lost their jobs when Blockbuster went bye-bye?

Maybe you didn't—but you must have been aware that the people you used to interact with—the ones who helped you buy stuff and things, were no longer employed there. And the building from which you used to rent movies or buy books is now a Chinese restaurant or CrossFit gym (true story).

You may have thought Pat's reaction to Devin retiring in my little tale was too cold and unfeeling. But let me ask you—as a former customer of Blockbuster or Borders or Circuit City, did you shed any tears when those jobs disappeared? When you're buying electronics on Amazon or watching *Orange Is the New Black* on Netflix, do you nostalgically look back at the days you needed to talk to someone who was wearing a nametag to buy a VCR or rent a movie? Nope. And neither do I.

So, when you read: "95% of Salespeople Will Be Replaced by AI within 20 Years"[1] or 93% of B2B buyers say that they prefer to buy online rather than through a salesperson[2] do you just chalk that up to fearmongering? Do you feel that people will always buy from people? Do you think our customers will push back against automation and AI and everything else and fight for the right to talk to a salesperson before they make a purchase (see Figure 11.1)?

Color me crazy, but I don't think our "Gritty Hustle & Hustly Grit" (trademark pending) will save us. Maybe you're feeling like Blockbuster employees did in 2003—that their jobs were safe because the only way Netflix could ever beat them was by renting people adult movies (also a true story).

FIGURE 11.1   *Source:* Courtesy of Derek Wyszynski

Maybe you work for a unicorn company, and like Family Video, you've found a customer base that will stick with you. But for how long?

U.S. Consumer Spending (in Millions)

Physical	Q1 2015	Q1 2016	YOY
Brick and Mortar Rental	$168.91	$140.20	−17.00%
Subscription (Physical Only)	$176.73	$140.70	−16.43%
Kiosk	$512.11	$409.45	−20.05%
Total Rental (excluding VOD)	$1,381.09	$1,258.83	−8.85%

Digital	Q1 2015	Q1 2016	YOY
Electronic Sell-Thru	$483.71	$505.01	+4.40%
Video on Demand (VOD)	$523.33	$561.48	+7.29%
Subscription Streaming	$1,188.98	$1,414.72	+18.99%
Total Digital	$2,196.02	$2,481.22	+12.99%

TABLE 11.1 Digital vs. Physical Spending Growth in the U.S., 2015-2016
Source: Digital Entertainment Group[3]

Here's the thing—something is going on, and we can't ignore it anymore. If B2C buyers are making purchase choices that cut out the need for salespeople, why are we as B2B sales organizations still investing in traditional, interruptive, sales-person-centric methodologies?

In English, you ask? Okay, smart guy. Why are we selling the way we don't buy?

Maybe all the caffeine I've consumed is giving me brain damage, but for the life of me, I can't think of any better way to craft a sales program than by first examining how people like to buy your products and services. And what the demise of Blockbuster, Borders, Circuit City, and others tells me is that buyers will always choose the least troublesome way to buy something. And I know from what I talk about—I used to be a buyer. (Dum Dum DUUUUUM—the big reveal!)

For the first 10 years of my professional career, I was in IT and IT management, and I purchased tens of millions of dollars of tech and software over the years, from salespeople—sometimes in spite of salespeople. You learn a lot about salespeople being on the other side of the table—if you're watching. A lot of good and a lot of bad.

At the turn of the century, I got into sales for many reasons—not the least of which was that I believed I carried with me the knowledge that salespeople weren't reading in their "how to sell" books.

You see, I was an IT buyer, so I hung around IT buyers. I joined IT buyer organizations. I went to IT buyer–related professional functions and mixers. We swapped stories about vendors and projects—I would say how I got my CIO to buy all new laptops and someone else would tell me how they got their CIO to buy a fax server. Sounds thrilling, doesn't it? Like a Hollywood after-Oscar party. Almost (see Figure 11.2)!

So, what was the supersecret knowledge I had that others didn't? The secret I knew was *I knew how IT people liked to buy*

FIGURE 11.2   *Source:* Courtesy of Derek Wyszynski

IT. Sure, I took tips and pointers from Solution Selling or SPIN or Zig Ziglar, but I crafted my pitch knowing how IT buyers liked to buy.

But like all secrets, mine outlived its "secretiness." Because IT people don't buy today like they did in 2000. Because they weren't yet renting movies on-demand and ordering a refrigerator while sitting in their underwear on their couch on a Tuesday evening.

You wanna know a prediction you can bet the farm on? We in the B2B sales profession will rue the day we ignored the signs of our own demise when we ignored the lessons of B2C.

Now you may be saying: *Boy, Derek, I read this whole chapter, and I am PO'd that your only take away was "sell the way you buy." You used a lot of words and gave me a big wind up and told me nothing I didn't already know.*

That's the whole point. You know this. You know the way *you* buy things.

You see, there's no asteroid coming to wipe out sales-people. The bots won't be the ones that get us. We're being "Darwined" out of existence. Two facts you need to know—from a July 2017 article on ShopifyPlus:[4]

- By the end of 2017, B2C ecommerce sales are expected to hit $2.4 trillion worldwide.
- That's a big number. But the truth is it's less than a third of B2B commerce's (growing) $7.7 trillion.

A wise man once said, if you want to hear what people want you to think about what they value, listen to them. If you want to know what they value, look at how they spend their money.

When Brian asked me to write this epilogue, I was honored. When he sent me the galleys of his book, the subtitle title he had written figuratively stabbed my eyes like the flash of a neon light that split the night (thanks, Paul Simon). It was this:

How to Change the Way You Sell to Match How People Buy
The way people buy. Not the way we learned to sell. Or the way we want to sell.

As soon as I read that, I ran to my computer to write something worthy of that insight. I hope I did him justice. Because I wholeheartedly agree with Brian; it's all about the buyer.

At the end of my little story, the buyer, Pat, embarks on a buyer's journey. Alone. Is it fiction, or is it a future yet to be realized? Again, I don't know. We'll all find out together, I suspect.

But one last thing. You've most likely heard the term "living in a bubble." The top Quora answer about what that means states:

> *Living in a bubble means you do not get out of your comfort zone . . . [many] parts of the world are outside of your comfort zone. But it is uncomfortable. You feel fear, awkwardness, loss of pride, anxiety.*[5]

In my personal experience, bubbles block out opposing viewpoints or opinions or even facts and make us uncomfortable. They cause us fear, self-doubt, even panic. There are political bubbles, social bubbles, racial bubbles, national bubbles—all kinds of bubbles. So many bubbles Lawrence Welk would be proud (those people reading this that are under 30 can Google it).

So what's the bubble we salespeople have chosen to live in? After all the words in this chapter, where is the lede? It's pretty radical but here is it:

We salespeople believe people like to buy from people.

There, I said it. No one that knows me can say that I don't, personally, hold myself in pretty high regard, but I'm also smart enough to know that if my customers could figure a way to get everything I can give them without dealing with me—a human salesperson—they would jump at it.

When I was at Xerox, a paragon of sales training and sales process, I had a Millennial customer ask me, *"Derek, is there any way to automate this process? I like you and all, but having you come in to sell me this technology is pretty old school—why can't I just buy it on a website?"*

This wasn't a one-and-done customer. This was a buyer who was responsible for millions of dollars of production print equipment for a Fortune 500 company.

As I look around my home office, I see these things I have—computers, furniture, artwork. Downstairs there's more furniture, there are cars in the garage, appliances in the kitchen. Outside, there's a huge trampoline for my daughter and a hammock for my wife. I have a shed full of tools and motorized whatsits to cut lawns and shrubs and even tree limbs. None of them—not a single atom—was purchased with the help of a salesperson.

So, am I supposed to forget all that when I put on my C-level hat and start begging salespeople to talk to me?

How to Change the Way You Sell to Match How People Buy

Brian's right. Pop the bubble. Change the way you sell. Or you won't be selling much longer.

Notes

Introduction

1. Wikipedia contributors, "Brian Halligan," *Wikipedia, The Free Encyclopedia* https://en.wikipedia.org/w/index.php?title=Brian_Halligan&oldid=7922 82207 (accessed August 11, 2017).

2. Brian Halligan, interview by Brian Signorelli. In person. Cambridge, MA, December 2015.

Chapter 1. I Was Never Supposed to Be in Sales

1. *The Digital Evolution in B2B Marketing*, e-book, 1st ed. (Arlington, VA: CEB Marketing Leadership Council, 2012), https://www.cebglobal.com/content/dam/cebglobal/us/EN/best-practices-decision-support/marketing-communications/pdfs/CEB-Mktg-B2B-Digital-Evolution.pdf.

2. *The Digital Evolution in B2B Marketing*, e-book, 1st ed. (Arlington: CEB Marketing Leadership Council, 2012), https://www.cebglobal.com/content/dam/cebglobal/us/EN/best-practices-decision-support/marketing-communications/pdfs/CEB-Mktg-B2B-Digital-Evolution.pdf.

3. *Gartner Customer 360 Summit* 2011, e-book, 1st ed. (Boston: Gartner Research, 2011), https://www.gartner.com/imagesrv/summits/docs/na/customer-360/C360_2011_brochure_FINAL.pdf.

4. Matthew Dixon and Brent Adamson, *The Challenger Sale: Taking Control of the Customer Conversation* (New York: Penguin, 2011).

5. "The Rise of Social Salespeople," *Forbes*, November 5, 2011, http://www.forbes.com/sites/markfidelman/2012/11/05/the-rise-of-social-salespeople/.

6. Gartner, Inc., "Gartner to Acquire CEB for $2.6 Billion in Cash and Stock," Gartner Newsroom, January 5, 2017, http://www.gartner.com/newsroom/id/3561717.

7. Sampriti Ganguli, email message to author, January 2010.

8. Brian Signorelli, email message to Sampriti Ganguli, January 2010.

Chapter 2. Why Inbound Sales Matters

1. Forrester, Inc., "One Million Sales Jobs Eliminated by 2020," Forrester Media Center, April 13, 2015, https://www.forrester.com/One+Million +B2B+Sales+Jobs+Eliminated+By+2020/-/E-PRE7784.

2. "Latest Inside Sales Research Shows It's All about the Leads," Ken Krogue, *Forbes Blog*, November 11, 2012, http://www.forbes.com/sites/kenkrogue/ 2012/11/11/latest-inside-sales-research-shows-its-all-about-the-leads/.

3. Mark Roberge, *The Sales Acceleration Formula* (Hoboken, NJ: John Wiley & Sons, 2015).

4. Aaron Ross, *Predictable Revenue* (West Hollywood, CA: PebbleStorm, 2012).

5. David Austin, "10 Things Sales Managers Should Know about Perform-ance," *Salesforce.com Blog*, August 21, 2013, https://www.salesforce .com/blog/2013/08/sales-managers-performance.html.

6. Brian Halligan, "Inbound Isn't Just for Marketing: Introducing HubSpot's Inbound Sales Methodology & Certification," *HubSpot Marketing Blog*, April 7, 2016, https://blog.hubspot.com/marketing/inbound-sales-methodology-and-certification.

7. HubSpot, Inc., "HubSpot Inbound Sales Methodology," accessed August 11, 2017, https://www.hubspot.com/sales/inbound-sales.

Chapter 3. Identify: How to Identify the Right People and Businesses to Pursue

1. CEB Marketing & Communications, "Align Sales and Marketing around a Common View of the Customer," *CEB Blogs*, June 28, 2010, https://www .cebglobal.com/blogs/align-sales-and-marketing-around-a-common-view-of-the-customer-2/.

2. Karl Schmidt, Brent Adamson, and Anna Bird, "Making the Consensus Sale," *Harvard Business Review*, March 2015, https://hbr.org/2015/03/ making-the-consensus-sale.

3. HubSpot, Inc., *How to Create Buyer Personas for Your Business* (Boston: HubSpot, Inc., 2017), https://offers.hubspot.com/persona-templates.

4. Robert Clay, "Why 8% of Sales People Get 80% of the Sales," *Marketing Donut Blog*, November 2015, http://www.marketingdonut.co.uk/sales/ sales-techniques-and-negotiations/why-8-of-sales-people-get-80-of-the-sales.

5. Mike Baker, "Should You Keep Calling That Prospect? A New Study Gives the Answer," *InsightSquared Blog*, July 28, 2015, http://www.insightsquared.com/2015/07/should-you-keep-calling-that-prospect-a-new-study-gives-the-answer/.

6. Sean McFadden, "Basho Strategies Inc.: Practicing What They Preach," *Boston Business Journal Online*, October 1, 2007, https://www.bizjournals.com/boston/stories/2007/10/01/smallb1.html.

7. "What Is the Best Time for Cold Calls?," *InsightSquared Blog*, February, 2014, http://www.insightsquared.com/2014/02/what-is-the-best-time-for-cold-calls/.

Chapter 4. Connect: How to Engage Active–and Not So Active–Buyers

1. Laurie Aquilante, "How to Prove the Value of Inbound to Your CFO" [Free kit], *HubSpot Marketing Blog*, March 10, 2015, http://blog.hubspot.com/marketing/inbound-marketing-cfo-prove-value.

Chapter 5. Explore: How to Properly Explore a Buyer's Goals and Challenges

1. Connor Burt, "5 Things Salespeople Do That Annoy Prospects," *HubSpot Sales Blog*, June 5, 2015, http://blog.hubspot.com/sales/things-salespeople-do-that-annoy-prospects.

Chapter 6. Advise: How to Advise a Buyer on Whether or Not Your Solution Addresses Their Needs

1. Nicholas Toman, Brent Adamson, and Cristina Gomez, "The New Sales Imperative," *Harvard Business Review*, March–April 2017, https://hbr.org/2017/03/the-new-sales-imperative.

2. Karl Schmidt, Brent Adamson, and Anna Bird, "Making the Consensus Sale," *Harvard Business Review*, March 2015, https://hbr.org/2015/03/making-the-consensus-sale.

Chapter 7. Closing and Negotiating

1. Dave Kurlan, "Do What's Not Comfortable," *The Kurlan & Associates Blog*, January 25, 2015, http://www.kurlanassociates.com/monthly-tips/2015/do-whats-not-comfortable/.

2. Personal Profile Solutions, DiSC Profile, https://discprofile.com/, accessed August 11, 2017.

3. "How to Negotiate a Sales Deal," Google Search, https://www.google.com/search?q=how+to+negotiate+a+sales+deal&oq, accessed August 11, 2017.

4. Joe Capiro, "The 5 Keys of B2B Sales Negotiation," *The InsightSquared Blog*, July 11, 2014, http://www.insightsquared.com/2014/07/the-5-keys-of-b2b-sales-negotiation/.

Chapter 8. The First-Time Sales Rep–to–Manager Survival Guide

1. Jason Jordan and Michelle Vazzna, *Cracking the Sales Management Code: The Secrets to Measuring and Managing Sales Performance* (New York: McGraw-Hill, 2012).

2. David Austin, "10 Things Sales Managers Should Know about Performance," *Salesforce.com Blog*, August 21, 2013, https://www.salesforce.com/blog/2013/08/sales-managers-performance.html.

3. Ibid.

4. Ibid.

5. Ibid.

6. Ibid.

7. Ibid.

8. Abbie Waite, "The Secret to Bill Belichick's Success," *The Lead to Win Blog—Intelligent.ly*, November 24, 2014, http://blog.intelligent.ly/2014/11/secret-bill-belichicks-success/.

9. HubSpot, Inc., *The State of Inbound 2016* (Boston: HubSpot, Inc., 2016).

10. Next Level Sales Consulting, "Motivating Good Sales People to Be Great," *Next Level Sales Consulting Blog*, n.d., http://www.nextlevelsalesconsulting.com/sales-insights/sales-library/sales-articles/motivating-good-sales-people-to-be-great/.

11. Dave Kurlan, "7 New Ways to Motivate Salespeople through 20 Old Hurdles," *OMG Hub Sales Development Blog*, September 8, 2014, http://www.omghub.com/salesdevelopmentblog/tabid/5809/bid/108195/7-New-Ways-to-Motivate-Salespeople-Through-20-Old-Hurdles.aspx.

12. Dr. Tony Allesandra, "The Platinum Rule: Do Unto Others as They Want Done Unto Them," The Platinum Rule Group, LLC, 2017. http://www.platinumrule.com/index.html.

13. Intelligently Management Training, 2017, https://www.intelligent.ly/about/.

14. Roberta Chutsky Matuson, *Suddenly in Charge: Managing Up, Managing Down, Succeeding All Around* (Boston: Nicholas Brealey, 2011).

15. Keith Rosen, *Coaching Salespeople into Sales Champions: A Tactical Playbook for Managers and Executives* (Hoboken, NJ: John Wiley & Sons, 2008).

16. Ibid.

17. Michael Shinagel, "The Paradox of Leadership," Harvard University Professional Development Blog, Harvard University, n.d. https://www.extension.harvard.edu/professional-development/blog/paradox-leadership.

Chapter 9. Reflections on Sales Leadership

1. Colbert King, "A Success Story in His Comfort Zone," *Washington Post*, December 30, 2006, http://www.washingtonpost.com/wp-dyn/content/article/2006/12/29/AR2006122901067.html.

2. Next Level Sales Consulting, "Motivating Good Sales People to Be Great," *Next Level Sales Consulting Blog*, n.d., http://www.nextlevelsalesconsulting.com/sales-insights/sales-library/sales-articles/motivating-good-sales-people-to-be-great/.

3. Dave Kurlan, "7 New Ways to Motivate Salespeople through 20 Old Hurdles," *OMG Hub Sales Development Blog*, September 8, 2014, http://www.omghub.com/salesdevelopmentblog/tabid/5809/bid/108195/7-New-Ways-to-Motivate-Salespeople-Through-20-Old-Hurdles.aspx.

4. Steve Jobs, Source Unknown.

5. Daniel Pink, *Drive: The Surprising Truth about What Motivates Us* (New York: Penguin, 2011), 108.

6. Phillipp Frank, *Einstein: His Life and Times* (Boston: De Capo Press, 2002), 185.

7. Karla Gutierrez, "Statistics on Corporate Training and What They Mean for Your Company's Future," *Shift Learning Blog*, January 28, 2016,

http://info.shiftelearning.com/blog/statistics-on-corporate-training-and-what-they-mean-for-your-companys-future.

Chapter 10. Sales Is a Team Sport

1. Hunter Madeley, interview by Brian Signorelli. Cambridge, MA, December 2015.

2. Kipp Bodnar, interview by Brian Signorelli. Cambridge, MA, December 2015.

3. Debbie Farese, interview by Brian Signorelli. Cambridge, MA, December 2015.

4. David McNeil, interview by Brian Signorelli. Cambridge, MA, December 2015.

Chapter 11. The Future of Sales: An Epilogue

1. Matthew King, "Why 95% of Salespeople Will Be Replaced by AI within 20 Years and Why Microsoft Will Beat Salesforce to It—Part 3 of 3 of the Changing Face of CRM," *LinkedIn Pulse*, August 30, 2016, https://www.linkedin.com/pulse/why-95-salespeople-replaced-ai-within-20-years-microsoft-matthew-king.

2. Andy Hoar, "Death of a (B2B) Salesman," *Forrester Blog*, April 14, 2015, https://go.forrester.com/blogs/15-04-14-death_of_a_b2b_salesman/.

3. Marcus Sanford, "In-Person Video Rental Is Dying. What Should Family Video Do Next?" *Business Clarity Blog via Medium*, July 3, 2016, https://medium.com/business-clarity/whats-the-endgame-for-family-video-996ffc48d62e.

4. Aaron Orendorff, "B2B Ecommerce: How the Best in B2B Sales Succeed Online," *Shopify Blog*, July 17, 2017, https://www.shopify.com/enterprise/b2b-ecommerce-how-the-best-in-b2b-sales-succeed-online.

5. "What Does Living in a Bubble Actually Mean?", *Quora*, April 13, 2016, https://www.quora.com/What-does-living-in-a-bubble-actually-mean.

Index

Page numbers followed by *f* refer to figures.

Communication:
  after failure, 166–172
  after success, 161–165
  B2B affected by mass, 180–181
  and buyer persona, 41–42
  HubSpot artifacts and examples of, 156–174
  in leadership, 143–144
  technology improved, 78
  and vision, 156–160
Comparably (website), xxvi
Compensation, 151
Competition, 83
Concession, 115, 119–120
Confidence, 42
Connect calls, 63–74, 77
  with inbound leads, 65–68
  mechanics of, 71–74
  without inbound leads, 68–71
Connect rate, 52*f*
"Connect" step, 63–74
  fear of dialing in, 64–66
  lacking inbound leads in, 68–71
  mechanics of calling in, 71–74
  opening line in, 66–67
Conscientious ("C") personality type, 111
Consequences, in GPCTCI framework, 79
Consequence questions, 81
Constant Contact (company), 14
Contacts, 47
Content, baseline, 69
Content marketing, xvi–xvii
Context buyers, xxi

Control, over sales, xxviii, 4–5, 24, 194
Conversion rates, lead-to-customer, 194, 198
Core business problems, 79
Core buyers, 48
Corporate Executive Board (CEB), 17, 64, 149
  and B2B sales, 92, 96
  and connect calls, 68
  and decision-making, 182
  sales and marketing alignment researched by, 38
"C" (Conscientious) personality type, 111
Credibility, 115, 180, 184
CRM software, *see* Customer Relationship Management software
Culture, team, 155
Customers:
  conversion rate for, 194, 198
  existing, 42
  good-fit, 37–38
Customer advocacy, 194–195
Customer Relationship Management (CRM) software, 42, 128, 182, 190

D
Databox, 26
Decision makers, negotiating with, 114
Decision-making, 5–6, 182
Delaying a close, 116–117
Demands, customer, 117
Differentiation, 42, 184